Eke Kingsley Chinedu

Child Abuse and Human Trafficking in Nigeria

Eke Kingsley Chinedu

Child Abuse and Human Trafficking in Nigeria

A Multidimensional indices for its resolution

JustFiction Edition

Cover image: www.ingimage.com

Publisher:
JustFiction! Edition
is a trademark of
International Book Market Service Ltd., member of OmniScriptum Publishing Group
17 Meldrum Street, Beau Bassin 71504, Mauritius

Printed at: see last page
ISBN: 978-620-2-48900-3

CHILD ABUSE AND HUMAN TRAFFICKING IN NIGERIA

A MULTIDIMENSIONAL INDICES FOR ITS RESOLUTION

BY

EKE KINGSLEY CHINEDU

DEDICATION

This book is specially dedicated to

Mrs carol Ndaguba

NAPTIP Executive Secretary

And

Hajia Mrs Amina Titilayo Abubakar

Founder women trafficking and child labour

Eradication Foundation. (WOTCLEF)

ACKNOWLEDGMENT

The decision to write this book comes from a deep- seated desire to properly sensitize and educate the Nigerian society of the danger of child abuse and neglect. Above all, the inspiration and perseverance to come from the Almighty GOD.

In my attempt to accomplish this work, I have solicited for and received numerous assistance from many people by way of advice, material, encouragement and even criticisms.

The first set of people is the numerous authors whose work referred to especially DONLI, H. N., the media and other institutions. I must single out for special thanks to Dr. Doreen Mulenga, Chief: protection and participation, United Nations Children's Fund (UNICEF) for this encouragement and providing one of the Last Comprehensive research Materials on women And children's rights in Nigeria.

If Children become in a sense a nation's Most crucial resource, then one has to pay much more attention to what happens to Children and to Families with Children" D. Bell

"Unless the investment in Children is made, all of humanity's most fundamental Long- term problems will remain fundamental long - term problems"

UNICEF (SLOGAN)

INTRODUCTION

The twin issues of child abuse and human trafficking have posed intractable social problems in Africa generally and Nigeria in particular. However, the aim of this book is to prove that these seemingly intractable problems could be resolved with a combination of social-psychological, economic and political indices of empowerment dimensions. Reason being that children generally, are assumed to be the future of any given society without which the future of such a society would be bleak.

A number of children face these ugly experiences annually. However, it is noteworthy that various forms of child abuse and human trafficking are hidden from the broader spectrum of the larger society, which this book attempts to expose. These twin problems of child abuse and human trafficking take place almost on a daily basis in our homes, social institutions, in the nation and across national frontiers and boundaries. The book also establishes a strong and umbilical relationship between child abuse and Human Trafficking.

In order to effectively achieve the above purpose, the book is drawn into seven main chapters.

Chapter one takes a look at the intricate relationship between the child, the family, neglect and abuse. Chapter two examines the different forms of child abuse Chapter three established and expounds the issue of human trafficking as a form of child abuse

Chapter four its part digs into the etiology (Factors responsible for) for child abuse. While chapter five indicated the consequences of child abuse and human trafficking.

In chapter six, the author prompts multidimensional indices for the resolution of child abuse and human trafficking in Nigeria – Africa.

Conclusively, chapter seven x-rays the models of pro-active crusade against child Abuse and human Trafficking in Nigeria.

Eke Kingsley

May 2005

THE MESSAGE OF A CHILD

You say that I am the future

Don't fail my present!

You say that I am the hope of peace

Don't induct me into war

You say that I am the promise of the good

Don't entrust me with the bad

You say that I am the sight of your eye

Don't abandon me to darkness

I don't want only your bread

Give me light and understanding

I don't only want the feast of your affection.

I ask for your love with which you educate me.

I don't ask you only for toys

I ask you for sound counsel and good words

I am not a simple decoration on your way.

I am a person who knocks at your door in the name of God.

Show me work and humility, sacrifice and forgiveness.

Be compassionate with me and orient me

So that I can be good and just.

Correct me while there is time

Help me today .

So that tomorrow, I don't make you cry

By Don Bosco San Jose Costa Rica

TABLE OF CONTENTS

Dedication 2

Acknowledgement 3

Foreword

Introduction 5

Message of a Child 6

CHAPTER ONE **10**

The child and the family

The intricate relationship between child

Abuse and child neglect

Child Neglect

CHAPTER TWO: Forms of child abuse in Africa **20**

Child labour

Child trafficking

Child rape

Child Prostitution

Inhuman slavery and forced labour

Child soldier – victim syndrome

CHAPTER THREE **29**

Human trafficking in Nigeria – Africa as a form

of child abuse

Conceptual clarification of human trafficking

A brief diplomatic History of human trafficking

The resurgence of Human Trafficking in the

20th/21st Century in Nigeria.

CHAPTER FOUR: etiology of child abuse **44**

Poverty

Obnoxious cultural/tradition

Broken home/family size factor

Juvenile delinquency

Crass materialism

War/violent conflicts

CHAPTER FIVE: Consequences of child abuse and human trafficking **55**

Psycho-social

Political

Economic

Health

CHAPTER SIX: The multi-dimensional indices for the resolution of child abuse and human trafficking in Nigeria – Africa **66**

Legal enforcement of the Basic Rights of the Child

The Legitimacy of NAPTIP in the control/prevention of Human Trafficking in Nigeria

Service delivery programs for victims

Effective discipline of a child

CHAPTER SEVEN: The models of proactive crusade Against child abuse and human trafficking in Nigeria 76

National Agency for the prohibition of traffic in persons and other related matters (NAPTIP): A role model.

Women Trafficking and child labor eradication foundation (WOTCLEF)

Rochas Foundation College

IDIA Renaissance

The Adolescent project (TAP)

Child Care Trust (CCT)

Recommendation 89

Conclusion 89

References 90

CHAPTER ONE

THE CHILD AND THE FAMILY

Who is a Child? " A child is a descriptive terminology for a natural person who is an offspring of another (either by birth or by adoption) and may also represent any human being from the moment of his birth (in a life state) until the attainment of the age of maturity! (Ayo: 1989).

According to the world book [2000]" child is anyone who is not yet an adult. From birth until sometime past the age 20 - the age at which most people reach their full adult physical growth.

A child, according to the United Nation Charter is a person within the age of zero to 18. It could be described as somebody that could not be held liable for all his / her deed and actions due to lack of maturity. Succinctly put, a child is a person between birth and puberty.

For the purpose of clarity, a child in this text is a young person under the age of 18 and not above 18.

THE FAMILY

The family is a group of individuals living under one roof and usually under one head. It is the basic unit of society having as its nucleus two or more adults living together and co-operating in the care and raising of their own or adopted children. The family forms the basic strand of the weaving of the national fabric. If every single family is happy and healthy so is the nation. If orderly and disciplined the larger society reflects that too. Hence the nation is the family magnified.(UNESCO,2000).

In another development, the new standard Encyclopedia (1986) stated that family in sociology is a group of person with close kinship ties, usually parents and their children some of whom generally live together in the same dwelling. A household may include persons who are not related to the others, such as servants and boarders, or may even be composed entirely of persons who have no kinship ties. Any group of persons living together as a family is often referred to as a family.

The above position of the Encyclopedia on the issue and the meaning of family goes to let one know that a family does not only mean people who are blood related living together under one roof. It all means that a family could be a group of people who are not related in any form; they may not come from the same place but live together in peace and harmony as one family.

The life of every child begins in the family" hence the family is the first agent of socialization. It possesses the natural right to provide physical, mental, emotional and spiritual comfort to the child. A child being dependent and highly impressionable is virtually defenseless during the first few years in life. At the birth of the child, family bestows on him social characteristics that significantly affect, what we think of ourselves and how others treat us, hence one family of birth largely determines one's place in the society. By the time the child acquires some independence and some sense of judgments much of the socializing work of the family has been accomplished. Childhood experiences within the family are likely to influence a person throughout his life. The ability of the family to discharge these functions determines the likely nature of the larger society.

Children play an important role in the family in all societies In some cultures, young women are or were not considered married until they become pregnant with their first child. In virtually all societies, children are cherished as potential assets. The presence of a child in the family guarantees the continuity of the family line. The parents must assure the basic responsibilities for protection, provision of a good health and adequate education, socialization, contributing towards social adjustment and eventual independence of the child.

The socialization process, which begins in the home, is complemented as children grow older by other institutions, such as the school, church, social groups and the media (Shepard, 1987).

Unfortunately, some families provide a hostile and an unhealthy environment for many children. Not all children grow up in a loving home; nurtured by parents who care. Each year, thousands of children are maltreated in some forms. Some suffer deliberate and willful injuries, others are passively neglected. Passive neglect cannot be quantified. (Shepherd,1987).It is within the family that children develop their personalities and self-concepts. Without the care and affection that are supposed to be provided by parents / guardians or other adults, children do not develop normally. They have low self-esteem, fear, are rejected, feel insecure and eventually find it difficult to adjust to marriage or express affection to their own children. Some young children who have not been given love and attention have become retarded or have died (chase,1975).

THE INTRICATE RELATIONSHIP BETWEEN CHILD ABUSE AND NEGLECT

Child abuse is a term that generally refers to the situation where a child is treated very badly by adults and most of the time those that are suppose to be responsible for him or her. This is the maltreatment of a child by a parent or another adult (world book, 2000). There is no standard definition of child abuse. However a narrow definition limits it to a threat to life, physical violence, including severe beatings, burns and strangulation.

A broader definition includes any treatment other than the most favorable care.(world book 2000).

Different people and organizations have given various definitions of child abuse. The African Network for the prevention and protection against child Abuse and Neglect in Donli (1986) defined child abuse as "the intentional, unintentional act which endangers the physical health, emotional, moral and the educational welfare of the child. These acts are those unacceptable normally to the community. In some cases, however, such acts include behaviors that may be accepted by the community but may endanger the well being of a child, although the child may or may not perceive those acts as abuse. Examples include sexual abuse, child marriage, child labor (exploitative) child trafficking, child abandonment, malnutrition and indeed physical abuse and neglect, therapeutic abuse and finally abuse and neglect of handicapped children (Ajibola, 1989).

Kempe (1962) defined, it as "a situation in which a child is suffering serious physical injury inflicted upon him / her by other than accidental means, is suffering harm by reason of neglect, malnutrition or sexual abuse, is growing without necessary and basic physical care or is growing up under conditions which threaten his physical and emotional survival"

Donli in Ajibola (1989) citing UNICEF defined it as "the portion of harm to children that results from human action or inaction that is proscribed, proximate and preventable"

Child abuse may also be defined as the cruelty to a child's physical, mental or moral well - being. It is willful acts involving corporal punishment, sexual exploitation, child labor, psychological torture and abandonment. It also includes deprivation, neglect and malnutrition as well as any action which prevents a child from achieving his potentials.

Child abuse is the physical, sexual or emotional maltreatment or neglect of a child or children.

More so, the Centers for Disease Control and Prevention (CDC) and the Department for Children and Families (DCF) define child maltreatment as any act or series of acts of commission or omission by a parent or other caregiver that results in harm, potential for harm, or threat of harm to a child.

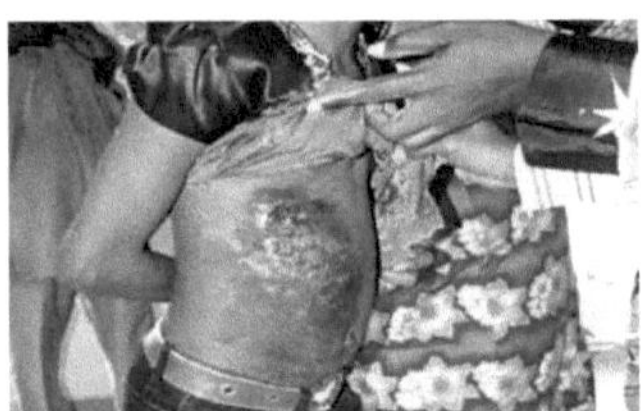

The issue of child abuse is complex. No one knows how many instances of child abuse occur each year, because many cases of child abuse are never reported., However, what may be termed Child abuse" by some people could pass for a severe punishment by others. The phenomenon is complicated when those directly responsible for the child turns to maltreat the child.

When a parent that is looked upon to care for the child turns against him, the child may see the treatment as normal and because the abuse or neglect may not come to the attention of people outside the home, until it becomes too late. Child abuse appears in different forms. A child may be beaten, burned, terrorized and forced to accept a series of very humiliating punishments or may be locked up in a room and starved for days. The child may be denied the basic rights of education and good health care.

Today, many experts believe that child abuse is widespread because society regards physical punishment by parents as a reasonable way of changing children's behaviors. Thus, adults who hurt children sometimes only intend to correct them and do not realize how easily children can be injured. What about the case of children being beaten with whips as if they are recalcitrant horses all in the name of discipline?

An example was revealed in Ebhodaghe (2000) article titled. " A man's inhumanity to a girl" he noted the incidence of a 13 year old girl named Chinaza Obom from The Lokpa Okigwe Local Council of Imo State. She was brutalized and nearly maimed by her brother in law, both live in Lagos State.

Chinaza was brought to look after the baby of her elder sister. The latter died while delivering a baby. The 13 years old girl, narrated her ordeal after being brutalized by her brother in law over a trivial matter. It goes thus."

> *On that fateful Saturday night, according to the girl, she was taken to a solitary place on Sunday and was brutalized. This was occasioned by the stain on the face of electric iron, which she was accused of. Here move my dress, as usual, tied my hands to the back, then I know hell was about to let loose on me, said Chinaza"*

She was beaten mercilessly with bruises all over her body. This is nothing but cruelty. According to Dr. C.C. Okeke in his lecture titled "The impact of cruelty and child abuse on the development of children: indicate this:

> *"If you are cruel to a child. You are abusing the child and therefore cruelty to a child is therefore part of child abuse"*

He stressed that a large number of African and Nigerian children in particular are on daily basis abused without any record of such cases. He further said that many cases are concealed, but available statistics show that l to 2 ascertained new cases per 1000 children on serious physical non-accidental injury to young children annually. (National post June 8 2000)

One may ask, what is the bonding between a severe punishment and an abuse of a child? In some developing countries including Nigeria, adults beat up children when they commit an offense or do wrong. This is because they think that beating or punishment would serve as a deterrent to other children and the child in question.

The most horrifying cases have been called the battered child syndrome (BCS). This is the willful and the unjustifiable infliction of pain and suffering of children. Indeed, this is cruelty done to children. Cruelty to children may be defined to include the failure to furnish proper shelter, nourishment or medical treatment as well as overt act of physical and mental torment.

The term battered child was used by Kempe (1962) to arouse public concern with the problem, but in more recent years the term 'non accidental injury has been preferred as being more consistent with a therapeutic rather than a punitive approach to the parents involved.

> *"Tuckwell mentioned as common place incidents following.... Biting a child's wrist till a wound was made and then burning, wound... Forcing the bony ring of a feeding bottle up and down the throat of a three month old baby till it bleeds... Leaving a baby of its cradle for weeks till toadstools grew round the child out of its own rottenness... Keeping the stumps of little amputated legs sore, to have the child with its little face puckered up in pain to excite pity. (Eekalaar, 1978)".*

However, attacks on children can coincide with severe cases of neglect. Apart from the obvious physical damage, children who survive these attacks have been observed as displaying a behavioral characteristic that has been described as frozen watchfulness. They do not respond vocally to stimulation.

But remain silent with a fixed star, an adaptation to the unpredictable behavior of the parent (Eekelaar, 1978).

As in the case of another form of domestic violence, it is very difficult to estimate accurately the extent of severe child abuse.

Many instances of non-accidental injury or as a result of a sudden loss of control by the parents. Shaking vehemently can be extremely dangerous to a young child. Injury can also be caused by failure to provide proper care for the child. In other words, even without inflicting such extreme trauma on a child, a family might fall to provide the input commonly considered necessary for the healthy rearing of a child. Children may of course be "deprived" in many different ways and deprivation is one feature of neglect.

However, deprivation is the denial of children, parental contact altogether. Their parents may have abandoned such children, either because they were unwanted or the parents were unable to raise them. In such cases, illegitimate children are the principal victims, they are both a disgrace and their future is without hope. However, some parents fail to provide sufficient needs such as food, clothing, medical attention and supervision. But it is arguable that personal responsibilities go further than that, and indeed that the major duty is to further the child's physical and emotional well-being, so that whatever is his endowments, he will have the best available opportunity to fulfil his potential in a society as a civilized human being (Eekelaar, 1978).

Child labor is another form of abuse.This can be defined as the unjust use of an underage child for economic profits thereby exposing the child to unnecessary risks which could be inimical to the life of the child. Such as use him/her as housemaid, street hawker, child conductor, etc.

Child labor according to NPC / UNICEF (2001) is meant by any work that is essential exploitative and injurious to the physical, social cognitive and moral development of the child. It further noted that child labor occurs when children, especially young ones, are exposed to long hours of work in a dangerous or unhealthy environment, with too much responsibility for their age and at the expense of their schooling. Furthermore, Child labor according to (World book 2000) is defined as the employment of children as wage earners. Some reformers began to condemn child labor practices because of their ruinous effect on children's health and welfare.

The most effective attack on the evils of child labor may have come from Charles Dickens novels Oliver Twist (1873-1839). Children worked for lower wages than adults, and were not so likely as adults to cause labor troubles. Factory owners wanted to use their small, nimble fingers for tending machines. Children worked for low pay in dirty, poorly lighted factories, mill and mines. They often performed jobs that really required adult strength(work book, 2000).

Many children engaged in this type of work to supplement the effort of their unemployed parents. These children are obviously unskilled laborers and are deprived of the chance to attend school. Children workers provide only unskilled labor. Thus, they had little chance to better themselves.

CHILD NEGLECT

What is child Neglect? Child neglect is the parent or guardian's failure to provide the basic physical and emotional needs of a child. It is the adverse consequence of inadequate or negligent parenting. It may be unintentional or inadvertent. When the neglect is deliberate and severe the term deprivation is used. For the normal growth and development of a child emotional attachment(bonding) must occur between the child and his mother as the primary caretaker. On the other hand, infants which are neglected or cared for in fragmented ways do not develop the trust or confidence in their ability or in the society around them.

Eckelaar (1978) asserted that child neglect might be an accompaniment to physical assault on a child which also might be so severe and as dangerous as direct attack.

TYPES OF CHILD NEGLECT

PHYSICAL NEGLECT

This is the type of neglect in which children are left under conditions of inadequate food, clothing and shelter. In most places, precisely the rural areas, children are grossly under clothed, neither fed well nor provided with comfortable shelter. They are almost always barefooted and exposed to the mercy of the harsh weather and diseases. They easily fall prey to pneumonia, malaria, and other diseases. Many of them go to school hungry with no provision of breakfast. These are common examples of physical neglect.

NUTRITIONAL NEGLECT

This is the neglect associated with a child's malnutrition and starvation. Most families cannot afford an average of two meals a day. The situation is so bad that some families hardly eat to their satisfaction, thus responsible for the poor health condition of children in most places. Malnutrition has made many children prone to diseases and has contributed immensely in retarding their physical and mental development, as they are either malnourished or undernourished. Singhal (1991) noted this when he stated that'' the negligence regarding nutrition may occur in one of the following situations.

(A) When both parents are working and nutritional requirements of the child are looked after by the servants.

(B) Disharmony among parents.

(C) When there is a female child and all the attention given to the male one alone.

(D) Too many children and thus not only is the care compromised, but there are financial constraints too.

(E) Children living in children's homes.

(F) Two or three female children in the family and everybody is anxious for a son.

EDUCATIONAL NEGLECT

Education plays an important role in the emergence of a progressive society. This is so because; it provides people with knowledge and skills that are necessary for development.

To educate children is to liberate them from the quagmire of Ignorance. Hence, it is the primary responsibility of parents / guardians. Some children are kept at home because of financial problems, as they take care of siblings, perform chores, a hawk on the street to meet their parent's financial needs. Most families have withdrawn their children and ward from school because of unnecessary reasons which include early marriage, learning of the trade, Hawking etc.

MEDICAL NEGLECT

This is the neglect that is associated with the child being neglected medically by the parents/ guardian. When a child is sick and could not be taken care of by the parents/guardians, the child is absolutely neglected. This carries the potential for a fatal outcome unless the intervention is vigorous and timely.

Singhal (1991) described it in the following way:

(a) Neglect in acute illness (parents do not acknowledge whenever an emergency arises, for example a child who is in shock and bleeding requiring transfusion, and a jaundiced newborn exchange transfusion).

(b) Chronic life threatening disease (Children with chronic disease e.g Asthma, diabetes etc. who experience frequent exacerbations or even emergencies as their parents ignore medical advice for their treatment) and

(c) Neglect in child health care. Example is the neglect of immunization.

This refers to the neglect and ignorance of most parents over the health of their children. Just as the immunization program is currently going on in Nigeria, every nursing mother is expected to participate with her child. Neglect of this program has resulted in the great army of polio - infected children in the country.

EMOTIONAL NEGLECT

It is not only sufficient to give a child the physical needs such as good nutrition, clothing, etc., the child also requires emotional feelings such as love, security recognition and praise. When such is lacking, the child is prone to some psychological problems such as depression, stress, aggression, unduly fearful, less self- conduct, etc. However, where there is love, security, the child is bound to grow into a healthy personally with self- confidences.

SAFETY NEGLECT

Safety neglect is the commonest among child neglect. It is a situation where an injury occurs because of gross lack of supervision. Children beyond the age of 4years are mostly unguarded and carelessly allowed to the hazardous home environment, which may lead to accidents. Leaving drugs, poison, knives caustics, guns, etc. within the reach of children is sheer negligence. Parents must supervise their children carefully in these early years as the highest morality from accident occurs during this childhood period. Most disabled or physically deformed children today are as a result of safety neglect by the parents/ guardian.

With regards to this, there was a story of a boy who killed his mother for her carelessness and negligence that led to the boy's lost on one of his eyes. It all transpired when the boy was a toddler and was left playing with a knife. Due to the fact that the mother over pampered the child, she allowed him to play with the knife. When the mother later removed the knife from him, the child started crying. Instead of leaving him to cry, the mother rather gave him back the knife, unfortunately, he struck one of his eyes with the knife, which the mother ought to have removed from him earlier. When the boy grew up, and was ridiculed by his mates, he quarried his mother over the matter, the mother narrated the whole thing to him, and the boy was infuriated and stabs the mother to death (oral discussion). This is pathetic. Thus, parents should be careful about the safety of their children which is their utmost responsibility

CHAPTER TWO

FORMS OF CHILD ABUSE IN AFRICA

In the African context, the place of a child is so important that a family is prepared to spend all its fortune in situations where there is a delay in the arrival of one. In addition, children are very important for the continuation of the human race. Therefore, they deserve all the love, care, devotion and attention from parents and the society at large.

Unfortunately, there is an increasing rate of child abuse and neglect in Africa. The issues of child neglect, abuse, child prostitution, child trafficking, child labor, etc. are most prevalent in the black continent. Children in Africa have been abused in different forms.

CHILD LABOUR

Many children in Africa and Nigeria in particular have been subjected and exposed to various negative implications of child labor. Child labor is a form of child abuse. Child labor is an unjust use of an under-aged child for economic profits thereby exposing the child to unnecessary risks which could be inimical to the life of the child. Such risks include the use of a child as a housemaid[domestic servant], street hawking, hackney business e.g. bus conductor, use of children in drug paddling and many others.

NPC/UNICEF (2001) defined it as any work that is essentially exploitative and injurious to the physical, social cognitive and moral development of the child. It further noted that child labor occurs when children, especially young ones, are exposed to long hours of work in a dangerous or unhealthy environment, with too much responsibility for their age and at the expense of their schooling.

Olawale (2000) in his article cited ILO description of "exploitative labor "as any work that hampers the normal physical, mental, social and psychological development of a child from meaningful adult life. All works capable of depriving the child of basic education, resulting in physical injury, jeopardize the health safely and normal development of the child is exploitative works".

Furthermore WorkBook (2000) defined child labor as the employment of children as wage earners. Some reformers began to condemn child labor practices because of their ruinous effect on children's health and welfare. The most effective attack on the evils of child labor many have come from Charles Dickens novels Oliver Twist (1873-1839). Children worked for lower wages than adults, and were not so likely as adults to cause labor troubles factory owners wanted to use their small nimble fingers for tending machines. Children worked for low pay in dirty, poorly lighted factories, mill and mines. They often performed jobs that really required adult strength (World Book, 2000).

However, many children engaged in this type of work to supplement the effort of their unemployed parents. This is because the economic status of many parents have been crippled by bad economic conditions which left some of them with no other option than to send their under aged children to the streets to help supplement the effort of the family in the quest to make ends meet. These children are seen on the streets begging for alms, while others do menial jobs and hawking. In some motor parks, children are seen working as bus conductors. Men drivers opined that they prefer children to adult in the bus conducting. The reason is obvious, not only that they take advantage of the fact that children are prepared to take any amount as commission; they are prepared to take orders than the adults while their lean bodies occupy only a small portion of the seat making room for more passengers. Thus, children are seen carrying different wares on their heads roaming along the streets. Some risk their life in pursuing vehicles in a bid to sell their wares in the highways. According to NPC/UNICEF (2001) report on the hazards of child labor on the streets of Lagos. It noted an eight-year-old Kuburant Ahmed, who nearly lost her life in quest of money. "There was risky business in the sachets of water, she was selling. She had sold the last in her small tray and when three passengers in an Oshodi bound bus asked for some, eager to make the extra money, Kuburant dashed across the road where she kept her stock of water. As she tried to run over again with the three sachets of water, an oncoming vehicle hit her. Luckily she did not die, but her injuries kept her away from selling water for several days.

The above report showed the high-risk measure of children who are allowed to hawk on the streets and highways. It is obvious that short children in Nigeria have dropped out from school and are left on the streets hawking, begging and working to eke out a living. The situation is a pathetic one as regard the condition of children in Nigeria. The United Nations Children's Funds new index for measuring development worldwide called the Risk, measures noted that the child with the highest risk in the world is found in sub Sahara Africa with Nigeria ranks high on the profile (Punch May 27, 2000).

HOUSEMAIDS/DOMESTIC SERVANTS

The institution of house help is as old as a mankind itself. Today it is regarded as a white-collar job. Most parents, their underage children to serve as house helps only to be paid monthly for the services, these children render. Domestic work is one among the hazardous form of child labor in the continent. However, there is a problem with the definition of domestic work because of its invisibility and lack of social and economic recognition. Though in most countries, it is not recognized as labor. According to Akinbode (2000) specific regulation for such work are in most countries either non-existed or not applied. The children who are engaged in it therefore have very few legal or social protections. They are exploited, ill paid and in some cases, not even paid at all. There are nor regulation regarding period of rest or holiday. These children can be dismissed arbitrarily and they usually do not have access to pension funds. Since this form of labor is common and traditionally inclined most parents allow their children to be employed as domestic servants or house helps either because of poverty or as a result of death of the parents, broken homes or as a result of death of the parents broken homes. Many cultures view it as an essential part or a proprietary enterprise, especially the female children for a future wife. These children are often recruited from rural villages through a family friend, relative and other contacts.

A study in 1992 showed that 75 percent of the 297 domestic servants between 12 and 17 years are from Akwa Ibom, Cross River, Imo Anambra and Oyo State. The Calabar people, particularly those from Akwa Ibom play the role of suppliers of domestic servants (Punch

These children under this service are often subjected to different hazards or abuse, depending on the person they are serving. It is obvious that many of them are not properly taken care of, to say the least; they are regarded as mere slaves. Some are deprived of emotional care and affection, beaten more than other children and more especially deprived of going to school. Most of them are subjected to various forms of abuse such as child hawking, child prostitution and exposure to danger of robbery and bad gangs and accidents that sometimes lead to disability or death. The female children are vulnerable to sexual harassment and exploitation that may lead to unwanted pregnancy. In some cases, most parents are ignorant of the hazardous and exploitative manner in which their children are being subjected to.

However, parents should minimize the number children they would have so as to avoid running away from their responsibility by nurturing their wards as it ought to be. It is glaring to note that these practices of house help or maids in an exploitative and hazardous way is a typical child abuse, hence it does not help the developments of a well-ordered society. The society and government should frown at child labor generally because the future development of these innocent children will be negatively affected thus affecting the development of the nation at large.

CHILD TRAFFICKING

The number of children being exploited through various forms of abuse is so high that something urgent must be done about the problem. The alarming rate of the growth of child trafficking activities going on around the boarders of different countries in Africa is of great concern to many people in Africa.

Human trafficking is among the largest criminal activities around the world as it is in relation to drug and weapon trafficking (Awake, 2003).

What is child trafficking all about? This could also be defined as the illegitimate act of taking a child away from the family with or without the consent of the child to an unknown destination for an economic value. It is the process where a child is removed from the parental protection and authority and becomes like an object of market value (Aina, 2000). It entails any action involving the recruitment, transportation, illegal reception or sale of persons, involving cheating, constraint or force bondage for debt or fraud resulting in the disappointment of the child within or outside the country (Yemisi, 2000).The reasons that child trafficking continues to flourish are complex and deeply rooted in the economy and culture of the region. In Western African society, it is surprisingly easy for traffickers to acquire children through trade. Some victims are kidnapped or tricked into accompanying their captors, but many go willingly or are lured by the promise of adventure and a new life beyond their villages.

Research reveals that child trafficking in the west and central Africa occurs in most countries of sub- region, including Benin republic, cote d Ivoire, Gabon, Mali, Ghana, Togo and Nigeria, (Yemisi, 2000).

This practice is extremely worst in West Africa. Some of the boys and girls that fall victims of this heinous crime are being used and exploited as domestic, unskilled workers, street hawkers, farm workers, plantation workers, hotel attendants and objects of sexual gratification, Because it involves migration from one country to another, however, it is usually viewed by both parents and children in question as an "elevation advancement process. This is commonplace among indigent families in Africa. These parents are conned by the merge amounts they receive from the traffickers. Some are enticed by the colorful stories they are told about the good life awaiting their children when they get abroad. This, however,it is not always the case (Yemisi, 2000).

Meanwhile, the decision made by the parents to part with their wards is based on a reasonable choice of the opportunities offered by the child's departure and not the risks involved. The decision often reflects high economic and social exceptions and is not based on a precise perception of the hazards that the child is faced with (Yemisi, 2000) . It is with regard to this, that Aina (2000) stressed that a lot of parents in Africa seem to deny the existence of child trafficking activities both within Africa and abroad. Unknown to most of them is the dangers these children are faced with at boarder crossings: the harsh molesting in the hands of the traffickers, even worst is the brutality from their expected masters'.

CHILD RAPE

Rape is a crime against a person. It is a crime of forcing sexual intercourse upon a person against the person's will, an offence, which is defined in section 357 of the criminal code as: -unlawful carnal knowledge of a woman or girl without her consent, or girl without her consent, if the consent is obtained by force or by means of threats of intimidation of any kind or by fear of harm, or by means of false and fraudulent representation as to the nature of the act, or in the case of a married woman, by impersonating her husband – (Woped 2000:4).

Child rape is a statutory rape; that is to say the seduction of a child who has not yet reached the legal age of consent. It is a legal one – which is based on the assumption that a girl who is under a certain age (12 to 17 years) does not have sufficient maturity and understanding to consent to intercourse. As such any adult male having sexual intercourse with a minor has broken a law, even if the girl child was willing participant.

In Africa, and Nigeria in particular, child rape has become one of the nation's most underrepresented crimes. According to Women's Centre for peace and development (Woped 2000). Rape is recognized as a punishable crime in Nigeria but as presently constituted, the punishment does not give enough protection to the female. This report shows that many women and girls have been sexually assaulted and many more will be assaulted if adequate measures are not used to tackle this ugly phenomenon.

The most horrifying is the rate at which children are being raped. Yet the incidence is rarely reported because of shame and fear sometimes by those who they trust and who should protect them, or by unknown persons, armed robbers, blokes, etc. Most children hawkers fall victims of rape on a daily basis..

Rape is a highly traumatic event which has a very negative impact on the child victim, and difficult to erase from the memories of children and is likely to remain with them for life. The victim experiences psychological distress, phobic reaction and sexual distinction, which hamper the full development of the individual.

CHILD PROSTITUTION

In many parts of the world, the problem of child prostitution is a frightening reality. This act thrives in environment where there is poverty. Prostitution is one of the oldest professions in the world. This is a highly organized criminal and decadent syndicate involving girls from the age of 7 to 15 in especially poor countries in the world. These teenagers are sent to other countries to work as prostitutes. Tourists from wealthy countries encourage this act of child prostitution.

Hence, this has become a profession to many young girls in Africa. According to Awake (200316): "Because of the high incidence of sexually transmitted diseases, such as AIDS, customers are willing to pay for higher prices for children who are considered more likely to be virgin and thus less likely to be infected" it further stated that' the fear of AIDS has caused men to seek ever younger girls and boys, which makes the problem even worse". Some parents sold their underage female children to these " flesh merchant" who export them to European countries for prostitution work.

INHUMAN SLAVERY AND FORCED LABOUR

A slave is one who is owned by another and deprived of most or all rights and freedoms. Hence the slave is dependent on the whims and the barriers of the owner, who may generally force him into any service and at least in principle, may even dispose of his Life. (Encyclopedia Britainica, 1994).

The 1926 convention on slavery defines it as "the status or condition of a person over whom any or all of the power attracting to the right of ownership are exercised. The criterion for defining slavery is the power of ownership, which is the ability of any individual to buy or sell another human being. Another criterion is where a person is so dependent on another that his or her most basic freedoms are subject to the other person's control. (Akinbode 2000).

The number of people forced into slavery around the world has risen to 27 million being a report published by an international human rights group. A similar study coincides with a special UN session on slavery showed that millions of girls working as domestic servants are forced into sexual slavery. The report further stressed that in Sudan between 5000 and 1400 children were abducted since 1983, while millions of girls are forced into domestic, worldwide, with hundreds of boys being trafficked to the Gulf to look after the camels. It is obvious that in African tradition, children are bound to obey their elders. Hence, the folks have the power to command their children who often are denied the chance of refusing (Guardian May 28 2002).

This has left children in conditions that one can best describe as modern slavery. In some cases, these under aged children are sold to brothel keepers and pleasure seekers (in the case of girls), This is also known as white slave traffic. Children are trafficked in the borders of most African countries, and are sold out to work in plantations under forced labor.

Perhaps more than any other thing, the boom in child trade has gone a long way to confirm earlier reports that this nefarious activity still flourishing in Africa. But what continues to fuel such trade has remained a matter of great contention. It is obvious, that the reason behind this nefarious practice lies at the parent greed for wealth and laxity. In the society today, and elsewhere, money answers all things and it does not matter how it is made. " Once you have it, you are covered". Of course, this does not say good about the society in general.

The question remains where is the conscience? These innocent young girls are sexually molested, and abuse when they get abroad. Research revealed that in sundry parts of the world, there are millions of young girls under the ages of 15 from Africa who are constrained to work as prostitutes. In many homes in Africa, some mothers have sunk so low as to force their underage daughters into national and international prostitution, which has earned Africa much shame and battered image. Some of these girls are made to lie with dogs and other beasts to the pleasure of their hosts, who pay them in dollars. It is pitiable that many African girls in Europe have thrown their woman dignity to the wind because of Dollars.

The parents who induce or force their wards into national and international prostitution never knew what their children are passing through and how they are making their money, such parents only concern themselves with the money they receive from them. It is quite pathetic and sordid that these girls after having sexual contacts with dogs and beasts are infected with different types of diseases that can wipe off a nation.

The question remains, who will be safe and where do we go from here?. Recently, there have been cases of African girls repatriated from European countries precisely Italy. Aina (2000) noted that some cartels and individuals exist who scout for girls to ship abroad on whose dirty money these 'vultures' feed fat. The girls are the losers in four dimensions, she stated, they sell their bodies to both men and beasts, the money is taken off from them by their investors(s)" what remains is sent home to greedy parents/ guardians and, most devastate, the life of these girls are permanently ruined, sometimes by deadly diseases.".The result of this act is always tragic. It is against this height of barbarous crime that a Brazilian Newspaper made open this sobering comment about child prostitution thus.

" Countries where such a practice is common, tolerate, accepted, and even sought after because of the [money] it brings experience every day the devastation

that it causes. Any Financial profit it may produce is inevitably annulled by the individual, family, and social disasters generated by such a practice". (Awake February 8 2003)".

Yet, despite the noble intentions of those who want to stop child prostitution, the problem is growing. What leads to this horrific situation? Why do so many tolerate or even promote such criminal activities?

CHILD SOLDIER - VICTIM SYNDROME

Children in most wars ridden African countries have suffered untold hardship as a result. They have been maimed, brutalized and victimized in different forms. These innocent children suffer more because of their impeccable and fragile nature. The use of children to fight a war is becoming increasingly fashionable. These children are abducted and enslaved. Children who are supposed to be in school, learning and developing themselves for the future are recruited to the armies to fight wars. This is the height of child abuse.

Moses Ebosele (200:15) in his article " Still a grim future for the African child" indicated from the UNICEF research that as of 1994 in Rwanda alone, not only did the majority of the children stay away from school, more than 100,00 of them (children) had been separated from their families by wars and ethnic genocide. He further stressed that in Angola in 1995,20% of the country's children had been separated from their parents and relatives by hostilities. The situation over the years has been compounded by the unabated civil war, which has torn the country apart, forcing helpless families to raise children in the most helpless of situations. He said most of the like their counterparts in other war- ravaged countries such as Liberia and Sierra Leone die regularly from preventable diseases.

In the similar vein, Mr Olara Otunnu, a special convoy of the United Nations (UN) secretary, General for children and Armed conflicts, in a Newspaper interview, Opined that::

" The children of Sierra Leone have suffered beyond belief, so many dimensions of victimization, the maiming of children including the cutting off of the legs. I met a child

who is now ten months old. He was 2months old when his legs were cut off. The sexual abuse of young girls from free town alone, we estimated something close to 4,000, children were abducted in January perhaps 605 of abducted girls were being sexually abused in some major ways".

He further indicated that massive use of children as child soldiers, which he estimated more than ten thousand persons below the age of 18 years who have been engaged in fighting the deep trauma of what children have experienced, the separation and displacement of families.

In Liberia the same dimension of victimization, brutalization, rape and recruitment of children in the army has been recorded. Many children who have been conscripted have subsequently been forced to commit atrocious crimes in their own communities, including killing their parents, relatives or neighbors. This has often been done to alienate the children from their communities- If they feel that they can never return home it ensure that they will remain in the rebel ranks (Jama, 2003)

Children from most other war ravaged countries in Africa like Angola, Burundi and Congo experienced these forms of abuse. Suffice it to say that the African continent is the worst affected by conflicts while in other countries, children are taught how to use the computer and link up with the world While in Sierra Leone, Liberia and other war - infested countries in Africa, children are being taught how to handle guns, grenades, taking of hard drugs to increase their killer instinct. Against this backdrop, Mr Otunnu decried that the responsibility erasing this act of abomination falls on the African people not on the outside world, and that the international community has its own responsibility as well. But the people in Africa, the leaders in Africa, the youths of Africa must rise and demonstrate an ability to help themselves so that the international community can help them better". (Punch, july14 1999).

Chikbok girls kidnap

On April 14, 2014, Boko Haram gunmen seize more than 276 girls from the Government Girls Secondary School in Chibok, Borno State. The girls are forced from their dormitories onto trucks and driven into the bush. Fifty seven girls manage to flee.

Boko Haram leader Abubakar Shekau claims responsibility, and vows to sell the girls as slave brides. The movement's self-styled "emir", Abubakar Shekau, has already promised to sell the Chibok schoolgirls into slavery. "Allah instructed me to sell them: they are his properties," he declared in a YouTube video released on May 5, 2014 shortly after the girls were swept away. "I will sell them in the market by Allah."

Shekau fills the internet with his ravings, many of which boast about how Boko Haram enslaves women. Boko Haram says they have converted to Islam and will not be released unless militant fighters held in custody are freed.

CHAPTER THREE

HUMAN TRAFFICKING IN NIGERIA- AFRICA AS A FORM OF CHILD ABUSE

Human trafficking is indeed an element of globalization, which the international community sneer at, therefore it has received condemnation at the sub-national, national, sub-regional and regional levels of the international system. Nigeria is generally regarded as a crucial country for the human trafficking trade, which is as a receiving country, as a country of origin, and as a transit route for traffickers. Human trafficking is a product of history, reminiscent of the infamous trans-Atlantic slave trade, although in a new fashion. One can rightly say that the human trafficking of our time is neo-imperialist slavery in the 21st century with its antecedent negative impact as well as a challenge to our polity.

Nigeria is a source, transit, and destination country for women and children subjected to trafficking in persons including forced labor and forced prostitution. Trafficked Nigerian women and children are recruited from rural areas within the country's borders – women and girls for involuntary domestic servitude and sexual exploitation, and pays for forced labor in street vending, domestic servitude, mining, and begging. Nigerian women and children are taken from Nigeria to other West and Central African countries, primarily Gabon, Cameroon, Ghana, Chad, Benin, Togo, Niger, Burkina Faso, and the Gambia, for the same purposes. Children from West African states like Benin, Togo, and Ghana – where Economic

Community of West African States (ECOWAS) rules allow for easy entry – are also forced to work in Nigeria, and some are subjected to hazardous jobs in Nigeria's granite mines. Nigerian women and girls are taken to Europe, especially to Italy and Russia, and to the Middle East and North Africa, for forced prostitution. (U.S Report 2010)

This chapter, therefore, aims at elucidating the cause, the mode of operation, its effect and finding a pragmatic solution to this seemingly intractable but surmountable challenge of human trafficking of our time.

In an attempt to give an adequate treatment to the subject matter, we shall examine the following thematic issues:

I. Conceptual clarification of human trafficking.

II. A brief diplomatic history of human trafficking

III. The resurgence of human trafficking in the $20^{th}/21^{st}$ century in Nigeria

CONCEPTUAL CLARIFICATION OF HUMAN TRAFFICKING

Human trafficking is viewed from different perspectives depending on the eclectic consideration of the individual scholars. Let us examine the word Trafficking.

According to Webster's Encyclopedia.

Dictionary (1995:1100) the word traffic denote

a) Import and export trade

b) The business of buying and selling

c) The passenger or cargo carried by a transportation system.

d) The movement (as of vehicles or pedestrians) through an area or along a route.

e) The vehicles or pedestrians moving along a route whereas. Trafficking denotes the act of carrying out a trade or deal.

The above denotations have generated several connotative definitions.

The united nation defines human trafficking as:

The recruitment, transportation, transfer harboring or receipt of persons, by means of the threat or the use of force or other forms of coercion, abduction, of fraud, of deception of the abuse of power or a position vulnerable or the giving or the receiving of payments or benefits to achieve the consent of a person having control over another person for the purpose of exploitation (United Nation cited in Dialogue April 2004 : 5)

The above definition entails that human trafficking has tri-dimensional features which including child trafficking, women trafficking and human smuggling

According to Anne (2000), child trafficking entails the process where a child is removed from parental protection and authority and becomes like an object of market value.It entails any action involving the recruitment, transportation illegal reception or sale of persons, cheating, constraint or force, bondage for debt or fraud resulting in the displacement of the child within or outside the country.

This definition outlines the internal / domestic dimension of human trafficking.In recognition of this, Ehigiamusoe (2004: 10) noted that there is the local version of which south – east – Lagos route is most active and notorious.

Ogundipe (2004: 13) was apt to say that:

> *Trafficking usually connotes trade in anything, when you do not have the proper official sanction by which you should do it. You can traffic in the currency, goods, or humans. In the case of women trafficking, we are talking about the illegal movement of people for money.*

Consequently, Oriakhi (2004: 7) in his own perspective sees the international human trafficking and prostitution as by – products of capitalist globalization. A situation in which the poor south (developing countries) with its emergent compradoral bourgeois class is simply responding to this demand of globalization of capital. The poor south has little or nothing to contribute to this elephantine globalization of capital other than migrant labor, which comes in the name of anything legitimate or illegitimate migrant labor

Olaniyi (2004: 65) viewing trafficking from the human rights /legal perspective said that for an accurate appreciation of the human rights issues associated with human trafficking and in order at sustainable solutions, proper understanding of the term 'trafficking and smuggling' need to be made accordingly. Both terms have been used interchangeably without clear distinction. Although, it has been acknowledged that the distinction between the two concepts is sometimes blurred, get, because they differ in theory, in particular in their human rights implications, a distinction is important.

Olaniyi (2004:65) continued that trafficking generally denotes the coercion or force movement of persons for the purpose of exploitation, with or without their consent. It is generally characterized by the subsequently exploitation of those trafficked. On the other hand, the smuggling of migrants usually relates to the facilitated illegal entry into a state in a voluntary capacity through the paid service of a smuggler. In other words, in the case of trafficking, the trafficked person is a victim, whereas the smuggler is regarded as a client in the case of smuggling. In addition, whereas smuggling is i considered to be 'a crime against state, trafficking is seen as a crime against a person.

The importance of the above distinction is embedded in the implication for the human rights of victims or clients of the perpetrators of these activities. For instance, it is argued that trafficking is an issue of migrant with human rights implication as it involve protection of individuals, whereas smuggling is an issue of crime and border control as it encompasses protection of the state.

Hence, unlike trafficking, smuggling generally has not been considered as a human rights issue. Whereas, such recognition of the rights victims of trafficking is welcome among human rights activist, however "it must be noted that smugglers often deceive individuals who have paid for their services. They often create a situation whereby those they have smuggled may be further victimized either directly or their relatives in the country of origin. This calls for equal concerns for victims smugglers"(Olaniyi 2004: 6)., Thus, there is smuggle- induced trafficking, this arises where the victims were deceived into believing that they were to be smuggled only to find out at the point of destination that they were being trafficked. Therefore, in most cases there is no clear distinction between smuggling and trafficking.

There is another school of thought that sees human trafficking as " sale and purchase of human beings (Obadina, 2001: 28)

In the words of Obadina (2004: 28) The sale and purchase of human beings and their use as unpaid labor with little or no human rights is not only a historical phenomenon but a current reality. The estimated 200, 000 African children sold yearly in Africa' modern slave trade is a lot more than the annual average number of Africans shipped during the four centuries of the trans- Atlantic trade.

Children today are bought in Africa, especially the west and central regions for as little as $10 each to be resold at huge profit to end – users in other Africa countries or outsides the continent. These enslaved children are exploited for work or sexually or both.

Having examined the above conceptualization let us briefly takes a look at the diplomatic history of human trafficking.

A BRIEF DIPLOMATIC HISTORY OF HUMAN TRAFFICKING BETWEEN AFRICA AND THE OUTSIDE WORLD.

In discussing the Euro- Africa diplomatic history, no issue generates more attention than the slave trade. All through slaves were among the items of trade in the trans- Sahara trade, in terms of numbers, it was nothing compared with the Atlantic slave engaged in by the Europeans (Osuafor and Njoku 1995: 34) prior to the actual trans- Atlantic slave trade slavery existed in Nigeria. For instance, that is to say after most inter- tribal wars, prisoners of war were sold off by warlords and chieftains of the various tribes (Amadi, 1982:43). None of the traditional exchanges of slaves were pervasive as the uprooting of the native Africans to other parts of the globe.

Mark Tetteh, a tourist guide at Elmina Castle in Ghana, quotes historians as saying that slavery began in a rather curious manner.Way back in 1441, a Portuguese, Antan Conclaves, and his crew on a return voyage to Portugal had stopped at a place called Reid' oro- place of gold, believed to be somewhere in today's Guinea (Conakry). Having captured 10 natives, he took them with him to Portugal (Akarue; 2004: 29). The reason that was adduced for taking these 10 natives were all shrouded in deceit.

Three reasons were given for this capture: to educate and train them to serve as interpreters for the Portuguese whenever they returned to Africa, to be trained as missionaries and to serve as souvenirs or proofs of their visit to Africa (Akarue, 2004:29).

Whatever reasons were given, these captives never came back. By the 1500s, the demand for West Africans to replace Native Americans in the Spanish plantations in the West Indies became part of Africa's sad story.

The actual Atlantic slave trade began with the Dutch when they had conquered the Portuguese colonies in the New World. Most important of these colonies was Brazil. The biggest problem of the Dutch was to find labor. A lot of the slaves who were in Sao Thome got transferred to work in the sugar cane plantation in Brazil. From 1637, the Dutch governor began to take all Portuguese ports on the West African coast, by 1642 this had been accomplished and the Dutch were the major suppliers of slaves in both Brazil and the New World. It is estimated that in the 1640s the Dutch Company exported well over 3,000 slaves to the New World. In the 17th Century, Britain and France entered the trade (Njoku, 1998:55).

The trade in slaves was primarily organized to satisfy European demands for cheap labor to work in the plantations in the New World, especially Latin America and the Caribbean. In Europe the goods were exchanged for items African wanted (like cloth, iron, gun and gunpowder). The traders normally would leave Europe down the coast to West African and exchange their goods for slaves. This was called the triangular trade.

On the coast itself the European traders made an agreement with local rulers and men of authority to bring them slaves. Sometimes a trust system was involved, which meant that the Europeans would not give the Africans the goods but promised to do so later. This brought in the element of trust and encouraged Africans to supply more and more slaves. The victims of this commercial relationship were domestic slaves; people who contravened the laws of their societies were sold into slavery. When African rulers discovered how wealthy, they could become by dealing on salves they devised other means, like warfare, to capture slaves. Other methods included kidnapping. By so doing, Africans become greedy and careless about human life, disregarding the sanctify of human life (Njoku 1998:55-56).

In confirmation of the fact that the slave trade is a specter of human trafficking, when the slaves were no longer needed due to the industrial revolution. It was finally abolished in the early 1870s (Akarue, 2004:31)

The impact of slave trade in Africa cannot be overemphasized. According to Figuerredo (2004:22) Africa was devoted by the slave trade, an integral part of imperialism from 1400 to 1800.

Offing (1980) posited that in the 400 years of the European slave trade, not less than 15 million Africans were enslaved in the new world. To buttress this point, the royal Africa shipped about 60,000 slaves from 1680 of whom over 14,000 died at sea. This implies that between the 15th and the 19th centuries, the African continent lost between 68 and 75 million people. These were the most vital part of the population, since the aged, the lame and the sickly were not among those affected (Njoku, 1995:37)

Other impacts of the trans – Atlantic slave trade include: disintegration of African societies, famine and starvation, destruction of ethnic solidarity as wars were fought to secure slaves, introduction of strange diseases by the Europeans that led to illness and deaths ,decimation of African military capability, uncertainty and fear; destruction of local industries, psychological traumas as the Europeans began to look down on Africans and African, began to accept their inferiority (Uzoigwe, 1973). Also, there were incidence of rape of the enslaved women, which led to the majority of mixed race people in Elmina, Cape Coast and other hubs of Afro – European contact (Ray 2005:57).

Above all, the slave trade left Africa is trailing behind other continents as a result of the affair – stated economic, psychosocial and political destruction of the continent. This has brought about the present intractable prostrate economy, leading to the eruption of the present day human trafficking in Africa, in the 20th and 21st centuries as we shall examine in the next section.

THE RESURGENCE OF HUMAN TRAFFICKING IN THE 20TH /21ST CENTURIES IN NIGERIA

The sale and purchase of human beings and their use as unpaid labor with little or no human rights is not only a historical phenomenon but a current reality. It is estimated that 200,000 African children are sold yearly in this Africa's modern slave trade. Children today are bought in Africa, especially the west and central regions, for as little as $10 each to be resold at huge profit to end – users in other Africa countries or outside the continent. These enslaved children are either exploited for work or sexually (Obadina 200 1:28).

The above is reminiscent of the 15th century slave trade. The only difference is that the Trans – Atlantic slave trade was formally and overtly organized whereas, the 21st century's human trafficking is covertly and illegally organized.

According to Aina (2000), research reveals that child trafficking in the west and central Africa occurs in most countries of the sub –region, including Benin, Cote'ivoire, Gabon, Mali, Nigeria and Togo. The practice is extremely inhumane, involving the exploitation of young boys and girls as domestic, unskilled workers, street hawkers farm laborers, hotel attendants, among others. Child trafficking is another serious crime in our society. Not a day passes without dailies reporting incidences of child trafficking. Children are lured into this act by vain promises, some are hypnotized while some are kidnapped and carried away to unknown places. These children are subjected to different kinds of in human treatments. In some cases, many of them were intercepted on board.

Olawale (2000) reported of 33 underage boys and girls who were being smuggled to Gabon to be sold out to work in plantations under the pretext of being helped to earn a living, these children aged between 11 and 16. He emphasized that some of the parents consented to such deals as a result of poverty. But nemesis, caught up with the traffickers when their boat developed some mechanical faults and mobile security officers rescued the children. He reported that there is no clear statistical data on child trafficking and that investigations reveal that the vice is thriving so much that it's prevalent in Akwa Ibom, Abia, Cross River, River State, Imo state and Ebonyi State. Abia state is said to account for over 5o% of human merchandise, Ondo, Osun, Oyo and Ogun states are other areas where child trade occurs, even as the agents operate between Nigeria, Benin Republic, Togo, Ghana, Gabon, Mali and Cameroon.

Most Nigerian underage girls have plunged into the business of smuggling themselves outside the country for the greener pasture through prostitution. Most of these girls are deported yearly from European countries precisely Italy. As such, it has added a more negative image to the reputation of Nigeria and Nigerians. Nigerian on the international scene has been classified as being notorious on this issue of girls trafficking. How does this tell good of Nigeria, when the society accepted the wrong values where the end justifies the means, and crazy quest for wealth and the worship of the rich.

The incidents of human trafficking of Nigerians to European countries and other places gradually escalated in the last decade. However, there was an increased speed in the recruitment of children and young women from a relatively poor background from Nigeria for 'sale' as a cartel. Nigeria occupied a central position when dealing with the issues of trafficking even at international level. Hundreds of girls are trafficked predominately from areas such as Edo and Delta States to European countries. On the South Eastern plank, most children are trafficked to other African countries such as Gabon on a daily basis, whereas, women in most Northern States of Nigeria are also trafficked to the Middle East especially Saudi Arabia (The Guardian 21 July 2000:61).

To attest to how this illicit trade in human beings has spread like wild fire in the country, parents who were battling with acute poverty resorted to withdrawing their daughters from schools on the promise that their children were going to greener pasture abroad. Thus, traveling abroad became popular in the most poverty – stricken home with Edo State alone recording up to 80 percent of those involved in this illicit business of commercial prostitution (Denis, 2004:11)

Thus, women, young women, young men and children are recruited by heavy traffickers in the pretext that they are sending them to work overseas and earn hard currencies whereas the underlying intentions were far from that.

In the last decade, there has been large scale trafficking of adolescent girls and young women in Europe, particularly Italy, for work in the sex industry. These women are lured abroad by traffickers promising them legitimate and lucrative work, but on arrival they are handed over to prostitution rackets. They are forced to engage in sex work to pay off large debts supposedly accumulated to pay for their travel documents, tickets and accommodation and to prevent non-compliance they are threatened with exposure to the host country authorities for possible imprisonment or deportation. In effect, these women are held under duress in the form of debt bondage. In a particular case, a young woman was told to earn 9 million Lira (about N500,000) from prostitution to purchase her freedom. By so doing, she wont have had sex with three thousand partners in the district of Rome to achieve her targeted sum (NPC/UNICEF, 2001).

Sometimes, the victims on arrival at their destinations in Europe particularly, have their travel documents confiscated by the traffickers to compel them to engage in prostitution, bestiality and pornography. Also, the traffickers to offset traveling costs to collect a specified amount of proceeds received by the victims. This ranges from $30,000 to $50,000 over a period of two or three years (Olagbegi, 200:61).

The craze to travel to Italy began in 1980s, when Nigerian pimps deceived some young Bini-girls into prostitution in Italy. When they returned with hard currency, which exchanged higher than the Naira, girls began to hassle both non-literates and literates alike (Newswatch, July 26, 1999).

Fresh revelations are made about child trafficking. The NPC/UNICEF (2001:210) indicated that children between the ages of 7 and 16 have been transported to Gabon and Cameroon from various points in Abia, Akwa Ibom, Cross Rivers, Rivers and Imo States, South – East and South South of Nigeria. Between March 1994 and January 1997, about 400 children were rescued in Akwa Ibom State, being one of the main departure points for Gabon.

In the North-West axis, 64, female were rescued in a container on their way to Lagos from Mokwa, Niger State. Although, the Chief trafficker claimed she had the full consent of their parents to take them to Lagos to be engaged as housemaids and hawking of groundnut etc. (Daily Sun March 8, 2005).

According to Daily Champion (2005) 67 women and children from a suspected human trafficking syndicate in a container was smashed by Lagos police command, apparently on a Journey across Nigeria's borders. The commentary said these kids and women are used for domestic service, prostitution, rituals, organ transplant and other forms of economic exploitation.

The above is true because apart from obtaining the consent of the parents of the children through deceit, children are also kidnapped from their parents. For instance, Nigeria sent back to Benin 120 children who were smuggled into the country for slave labor breaking stores at quarries. The children, aged between 4 and 13, had been kidnapped from their parents. A first group of 116 children, aged 10 and 12, was repatriated in September 2003. The second batch was sent back in October 2003. Six (6) Benin nationals and three Nigerian were arrested for changes of child trafficking (Africa today, November 2003:16).

The Nigeria authorities say up to 6,000 enslaved children could be repatriated to Benin Republic in the succeeding months. Police sources say the children were found living in crude camps in the bush in terrible conditions in Ogun, Osun and Oyo States in South Western Nigeria. They were malnourished and slept in the open and at least 13 of their companions had died between September and November 2003 (Africa Today, November 2003:16).

However, this atrocious and dastardly act of human trafficking is not perpetrated in a vacuum: Many factors are responsible. They include:

(a) Cultural values and practices;

(b) Poverty

(c) Materialistic value orientation;

(d) Ignorance;

(e) Greed

(f) Low self – esteem

(g) Parasitic value system

(h) Unemployment

(i) The logics of capitalist imperialism

(j) Corruption

(a) CULTURAL VALUES AND PRACTICES:

There are social values and cultures that increase or decrease human capacity to enhance his freedom and material well being. A society that denies free will on the basis that humans are constrained by some form of determinism – birth, caste, race, religion, etc. suppresses people's potential for creativity and their ability to shape their future. The practice of virtually owing another person's labor or paying slave wages for personal services is not unusual in the continent. In some respects, it is this customary behavior in Africa that has gone global with children not dispatched to nearby relatives and 'big men,' but to strangers and sometimes relatives in far away countries (Obadina 2001:29).

Also, traditionally, women have been using their female children to gain wealth and in the Bini culture, for example, this is not frowned on but admired. This is not a question of promiscuity, but rather a matter of attitude. Bini women are also socially freer in terms of marriage unlike most cultures. Bini women could build their own houses, although married (Ogundipe, 2004:6)

(b) POVERTY

One of the major motivating factors to human trafficking is poverty. Child trafficking is viewed as an elevation or a way of reducing poverty in homes by the non-literate and poor parents. These parents are deceived by the colorful stories and empty promises made to them by the traffickers as well as by the meager amount they received from the trafficker.

(c) MATERIALISTIC VALUE ORENTATION:

This arises from the problem of falling standard in values. In the ancient past, it was very rare and unimaginable for somebody to get involved in evil dealings at the expense of others or for success to be measured with the number of cars, buildings, gold or other materials one possesses. It is a different story today. Titles and respect, awards and honors are only reserved for those who are wealthy, not minding how the money is acquired. Nigerians adore whoever is wealthy; the source of the wealth does not matter.

(d) **IGNORANCE**

The girls are lured with promises of non-existent job abroad. There is a strong belief that none of the parents who understand the kind of dehumanizing treatment these girls or boys are made to undergo will allow their wards to travel. The reason trafficking is deep rooted in Nigeria is because traffickers were able to hoodwink the local communities into believing their spurious stories.

In the word of Aina (2000) the decision of parents to hand over their children to traffickers often reflects high economic and social expectations and is not based on a precise perception on the hazards that the child is faced with.

(e) **GREED**

Closely knitted to materialistic tendencies is greed. Those who want to make quick money overnight are the traffickers and their victims alike. The false lure of foreign currency and quick riches has continued to blind youth who are desperate to engage in clandestine business of sex trade and human trafficking. It is also worrisome that many greedy parents are still pressuring their children into indulging in crime (Dennis, 2004:11).

(f) **LOW SELF – ESTEEM**

Victims of trafficking are mostly people who are disaffected with their life rightly or wrongly. They think that the so-called green pastures with wonderful Opportunities exist everywhere in Europe. Thus, they hardly listen to the details of the conditions before traveling there.

(g) **PARASITIC VALUE SYSTEM**

Although, the depressing economic situation in Nigeria might have forced several women from poor homes into the act of trafficking instead of finding other means of livelihood, parents of those trafficked have jettisoned hard work and have solely depended on their daughters abroad to send money home to cater for their basic needs. This is most debasing and parasitic attitude that encourages, human trafficking. There are clear examples of this dastardly act as portrayed by two horrific and sordid stories contained in the Newswatch. Writing on a cover page titled "Sex Export" the Newswarch (1999) portrayed vividly the story of a child prostitute induced by the mother in the Benin City capital of Edo State.

"It reads thus: Itohan Amazon (Real names changed to protect her); a 15 year old virgin, who lived with her mother at Ogbeide Street Benin was determined to complete her Secondary School education last year (being 1998). But her mother had a different plan. She wanted her to go to Italy instead to "do work", a euphemism now popular in the Benin capital of Edo State, for the booming sex export trade. Emmaseun is from a family of five , Her father died in 1997.Her mother kept the family going with what she earned by selling roasted plantains at Uselu market. She considered sending her daughter to Italy as the surest way out of the problem the family faced. But Emmasuen refused to go to Italy to work.

The Newswatch gathered that one morning in Benin, her mother tongue- lashed her and threw her out of the family home.

Though angered by her mother's action, Emmasuen walked back to her, hours later, to say she was ready to do her bidding and go to Italy. Her sponsor, as the "flesh merchants" are called, was Osahon, a man in his middle 40s. He specialized in procuring young girls for prostitution in Torino and Palermo in Italy. Amazons mother pledged the late husband's plot of land and only has to Osahon as collateral. The daughter was, as required, to pay an Osahon certain amount of money later in Italy.

The Virgin girl was also forced to take an oath that would forbid her making trouble with either her sponsor or her "host" in Italy. The oath was prepared with her pubic hair, one of her underwears and her finger and toe nails. She also fulfilled two other concoction. Osahon used her as a house girl for one month and slept with her to perfect her. "Perfecting" a recruit is a standard rule, if the sponsor is a man. It further stated that Emmasuen wept bitterly the day she was deflowered by her sponsor. But the mother consoled her by painting a very rosy picture of how the family's life would soon change for better, for just that single sacrifice the daughter had made. She would build houses in choice areas of Benin and become herself a landlady like her mate's in town. Her brothers and sisters would live well and get a good education. And she, the mother would also become a proud owner of Jewelry expensive wrappers.

It was observed that Emmasuen later went to Italy for prostitution. Some Some parents have to be blamed on their attitudes towards their children.

Many of them have thrown dignity and honor to the wind just to become one thing or the other. Money is not the end of everything in life. This girl was forced to sacrifice her precious life to redeem other members of the family. In fact, this act has led many young girls to their early grave. Some have been reported dead, others came back with sundry diseases that are beyond medical diagnosis.

The same News watch (1999) reported of a young girl who fell victim by contacting diseases that are beyond medication. The brother of this girl testified thus:

"'We sold our father's house together with his tomb to send her to Palermo. She was there for three years. But could not come back with anything. Her mates were bringing home buses, cars and other good things, but she chooses to bring home one strange illness. There was warts and craw craw all over her body. We have spent over N50,000 treating her without success. We will soon ask her to vomit all the money. She told me two secrets., she said a rival harmed her with black magic. She also admitted that dog had sex with her.Now she is at a witch doctor's place where we are still trying our last help to her.

What a sordid experience! Parents always see the benefits they would derive from their daughters who are prostituting abroad, but are blind to see the danger inherent in it. Life is very precious and must be guided with every amount of carefulness. Many of these girls are killed in the course of their business. In spite of the problems, some girls keep on smuggling themselves outside of such business abroad. If this menace is not curbed now, the society will be in danger.

(h) **UNEMPLOYMENT**

Unemployment contributes to human trafficking when almost half of the population is employed citizens are prepared to do anything humanly possible to survive hardships. The recession in the Nigerian economy, leading to mass unemployment and retrenchment of workers as well as high cost of living has accentuated poverty in the land. In order to survive therefore, some families even now encourage their young women and children to undertake the trip.

(i) **THE LOGICS OF CAPITALIST IMPERIALISM**

According to Oriakhi (2004 :7) unless we understand the forces and the spirit behind the drive for primitive accumulation in capitalism, we cannot appreciate why international prostitution and human trafficking which in contemporary times are, money spinning trades, will continue to thrive. It is a "functional" fall –out of capitalist globalization. The trade will continue to boom because capitalism is "fetish" in all its ramifications. It had no humanistic commitments. What is important to capitalism is the clearing out, and consequently appropriation of surplus. The ever poor countries of the South (Nigeria inclusive) have nothing tangible to contribute to capitalist globalization apart from a vast chest of largely untrained human resources, who largely remain pitchers of water and hewers of wood in the world of capitalist hegemonies, dominated by the United States.

(j) Corruption

The context in Nigeria formed by decades of military regimes, leading to severe political, social and economic crises, is fundamentally a contributory factor of human trafficking. First of all, although Nigeria is rich in natural resources, political instability and widespread

Corruption has facilitated trafficking in persons and

Hampered the progress towards reducing poverty. Nigeria is plagued by corruption at every level of society. The high level of corruption in Nigeria makes it possible for unscrupulous persons to use official channels to secure bogus travel documents for new recruit into prostitution abroad. Sometimes there is corruption even within the foreign missions themselves making it possible for criminals minded persons to procure visas for a fee. Nigeria has attained a global status in corruption.

This submission found its support from a recent report by transparency international which tagged Nigeria as the 38h most corrupt nation in the global rating.

A 2015 report by Human Rights Watch noted that Endemic public sector corruption continued to undermine the enjoyment of social and economic rights in Nigeria. Corruption can facilitate trafficking, for instance, it can ease the transportation of victims within countries and across borders without detection or requests for paperwork.Economically disempowered and destitute families, aiming to escape poor conditions of living, are vulnerable to traffickers. Women and young girls, owing to feminization of poverty and discrimination, cultural practices, are even more exposed to the tactics of traffickers

Secondly, the political system characterized by institutional weakness and fragility, has created Fertile ground for organizing criminal groups to thrive.

According to the 2015 United State Trafficking in Persons

Report13, "EUROPOL has identified Nigerian organized crime related to trafficking in persons as one of the greatest law enforcement challenge to European governments."

Finally, following the oil boom in the 1970s, opportunities for migration, both inside and outside

The country, created avenues for exploitation and international trafficking14

CHAPTER FOUR

AETIOLOGY OF CHILD ABUSE

POVERTY

Poverty has been identified as one of the factors responsible for child abuse and neglect in the society. The UNICEF information and public Affairs officer, Dr Adebayo Fayoyin identify poverty:

"As generally the major cause of child trafficking and child labor and that everybody is corned about the survival strategies. Hence the general Opinion might be that children should be allowed to work and earn money so as to reduce the burden that their parents have to bear. But considering the consequence. Or outcome of street trading or hawking .It might not be worth the while (Olawale 2000).

In the same vein, the UNICEF Regional Adviser for east and southern Africa identified the remote causes of child abuse and neglect in Africa. "As structural in qualified, diseases, draught, armed conflict and political violence. These remote causes necessarily lead to abject poverty, death of parents, abduction of parents military conscription of children, physical abuse and torture as well as deliberate and accidental deaths.(Ajibola, 1989)

Aina (2000) also indicated that: "Some of the causes of child trafficking has been analyzed to include the high level of poverty in African cultural valves and practices, unaware of the risks involved, insufficient training and educational opportunities, desire of child to migrate in search of economic and social well being (i.e. The get rich quick syndrome in Nigeria) high demand for cheap labor, and the inadequate or nonexistence of national legislation on child trafficking."

From the foregoing, it is obvious that poverty is a major factor responsible for child abuse and neglect. In a situation where there is poor quality of life, unemployment, the adverse economic environment and abject poverty and the parents, there is a high likelihood of a child trafficking, neglect from such circumstances, the children are exposed to hazardous labor and other forms of abuse just to make ends meet. According to NPC/ UNICEF(2001) poverty prevents many families from enrolling all or some of their children in school or forces them to withdraw their children prematurely from school, because of the cost of education or the need to put children to work, either within or outside. In the similar vein, Oloko (1990) appraised that " it is no longer rare to see children as young as six or seven years old hawking. Specializing mainly in the sale of iced water in motor parks at bus stops and in go - slows on busy urban highways, they are at high risk of accident at this very young age" .The female ones fall victims of sexual abuse that sometimes results in early pregnancies and prostitution.

The high rate of child abandonment along the streets, gutters and dustbin are as a result of poverty. The mother of these babies deliberately abandons them mainly because they cannot fend for themselves.

According to Donli in Ajibola (1989). "A survey of Nigerian National Dailies indicates that child abandonment is the most frequently reported form of child abuse and neglect, forming an average of 25% of reported of child abuse and neglect from the data gathered. Most of them were dumped in the gutter, pit latrines rubbish dumps, bush or pathways never the bush. Some were also abandoned near places like police stations and hospitals where they might be found and taken care of. This set is mostly abandoned by the low income women who cannot afford to fend for the child".

This wicked act is prevalent among schoolgirls, students, prostitutes and young mothers. This is predominantly done where the child is born out of wedlock or denied. This vividly ascertained that poverty has been the prevailing factor and has a far reaching implication in the problem of child abuse and neglect in the society.

OBNOXIOUS CULTURE / TRADITION

The culture is peoples way of life, which include their habits, custom etc. There are "unpleasant and "uncivilized customs that adversely affect the people. Some aspects of our culture and tradition are true sources of child abuse. Most of these unwholesome traditions have been abolished while some are still in practice. Both old and present practices are inimical to the development of the child.

Fortunately, the case of killing twin babies regarding them as a bad omen and the abandonment of a child who has its first milk teeth in the upper jaw in the thick forest, have all been wiped out. This is sheer infanticide and gross form of child abuse.

Female circumcision is one of the unwholesome traditional practices that is still in practice. It is known as genital mutilation. Female circumcision still remains one of the most divisive and controversial cultural fissures that continues to attract revulsion across the globe. This is the surgical removal of the clitoris and labia that remain a rite of passage for girls throughout Africa. According to NPC/ UNICEF (2001) the practice of female circumcision, which is now widely known as female genital mutilation (FGM), is one of the most serious forms of violence against women. It further noted the world Health Organization (WHO) defined as "all procedures which involve partial or total removal of the external female genitalia and/ or injury to the female genital organs, whether for cultural or any other non - therapeutic reasons". It is a common practice deeply rooted in tradition. The most severe form is called infibulations. This is the removal of the clitoris, labia minora and part of the labia majora, which are then sewn shut. This has a lot of medical risk and has led many women today into some gynecological problems in different ways.

Early marriage is another cultural practice that endangers the life of young children. In some parts of Nigeria, this practice is common. Some parents withdraw their children from school without their consent and give them in marriage to older men who are suppose to be their fathers. According to NPC/ UNICEF (2001) a huge number of girls are married off by their parents in their early teens, when they are too young for their consent to be sought or given. In many cases, they are married to much older men sometimes man old enough to be their fathers or even grandfathers. This practice is predominant in the Northern Nigeria. In this sense, Early child married, has also been found to be associated with this form of diseases. Early childbirth leads to maternal mortality or morbidity. According to favoring (1993) research shows that several thousand young girls in Nigeria are getting pregnant and becoming mothers at a ridiculously early age. Half of all women surveyed were married by 17 years. He further noted that practical experience in several parts of the country; young girls between 11 and 15 years become mothers. Many of them are pupils withdrawn from school and married far older men. Mallam Kaita (1969) in his paper, revealed that the case of early child marriage is very common in the far north both in the urban and rural areas. A girl may sit for the common entrance examination and get admitted to a secondary school after doing very well in her examinations. Her parents may decide to withdraw her from going to further study, in this case, she is forced by local custom to get married at the age of twelve or thirteen sometimes to an old man. Of course at this stage the girl has not yet developed or matured enough to shoulder her home responsibilities nor is she ready to bring up her own children. She is, after all, a child herself, requiring parental care and guidance. If the girl is lucky enough the marriage may last long, but the unfortunate ones get a divorce after a short while. In this case her opportunities have been destroyed. She has missed the chance of furthering her education and this sometimes upsets her peaceful life. This could even lead the poor young girl to become a prostitute, Thus her future is ruined.

In addition to this, Ebigbo (1993) indicated that the Moslem religion does not allow female children to get pregnant without being married. It recommends that in order to avoid this, a girl should be at the husband's home latest by the second menstruation. However, this practice has sent many female children to their grave, while some have been impaired for life. The detrimental effect of this form of abuse on children is the medical complications experience during childbirth. According to Zabin and Kiragu in NPC / UNICEF (2001) early pregnancy is likely to be one of the main reasons for the much higher maternal mortality and greater prevalence of conditions such as VVF/RVF in northern Nigeria. They further noted that Research in Zaria has found that maternal mortality among women aged 20-24. NPC /UNICEF (2001) noted that VVF arises from obstructed and prolonged labor. When an under -aged girl goes into labor, her pelvic bones are not yet sufficiently developed to allow the passage of the baby's head. As a result of fetal head presses on the surrounding tissues and organs. If this continues for long, the pressure can lead to fistula, in the form of holes between the bladder and vagina (VVF) and in extreme cases between the vagina and the rectum (RVF). This harmful practice does not only violates the CEDAW child's rights, but leaves the victims of trauma and agony for the rest of their lives.

More so, many teenage girls who objected to this practice have been subjected to various forms of dehumanization and subsequently died. The case of Hauwa Abubaka still remains fresh, as this topic is concerned. Hauwa was a child wife who died an undeserved death at the age of 12; her parents gave her in marriage against her wish on March 4,1987. She objected to it and her so-called husband chopped off her legs to prevent her from running away and she died as a result of the pains. In another development, there was a case of 14 - years old girl by name Uwala who was bathed with acid for refusing to marry a man enough to be her grandfather According to Osauzo (2003) Uwala was severely deformed as she was pouring acid on that fateful day of April 21st in the midnight while she was asleep for refusing to marry a 41 year - old man. In addition, there are some traditional therapeutic abuses of children in the society. According to Donli in Ajibola (1989) this involves therapy that is harmful and produced adverse or no healing effect, for example, burning the sole of the feet of a convulsing child, the carving of deep tribal marks on the face, female circumcision, the incidence of Almajiri etc.

In the light of the above, there is every need for the society to rise up against these practices as much as it contradicts the fundamental human rights of children, which eventually leads to dehumanizing treatments and death on children. A step in this direction should be one of the highest priorities.

FAMILY SITUATION

It is obvious that divorce, separation and death of one or both parents are contributory factors in the problem of child abuse and neglect. Many children brought up in broken homes are likely to be abused and neglected. Such children grow up to become abusive parents. A child is abused absolutely if he/ she is not well taken care of by the parents. A child may be emotionally abused by the mere fact of divorce and may become neglected due to diminished parental care.

Meanwhile, if a child is properly brought up in a peaceful home, where love and affection reign, that child must be satisfied emotionally. This could only exist where both parents are in good terms and in harmonious relationship. A situation where parents have not much time to spend with their children affects the children and is therefore a form of neglect. The common neglect of children in urban areas is inattention. Many parents are preoccupied with their own avenues of escape from reality. They are little listening to and being with their children. When parents devoted much of their time to business , work or in the unreasonable and greedy rate race for wealth, with little regard to the emotional and overall well being of their child, the child is susceptible to abuse.

Most parents leaves the welfare of their children in the hand of housemaids or house helps, however, efficiently they may be such maids who cannot play the role of parents. It is not all housemaids and house helps that are interested in the welfare of the children under their care. On the ay in addition, be abused to death.

Children who lost both parents are prone to be abused in our society. Stepparents or orphanages and foster homes are last hopes to such children. It is obvious that a child that is nurtured by the stepparents or foster homes lacks good welfare packages.

Since the child is not its own child, the treatment the child receives would be harsh and pathetic. He /She would be subjected to an undue hardship. He / She has no option when anything is demanded of him. In fact, the condition of such a child is better imagined than experienced He would be withdrawn from school and sent hawking to feed himself and even the entire family. Unfortunately, today many Nigerian children are under this condition but undetected.

The size of the family is another factor responsible for the abuse and neglect of children. In the African traditional settings polygamous families exist. This is where a man married more than one wife. It is believed that multiples of children in the family constitute a man's prestige.

In Chinue Achebe (1958) "Things fall apart" he succinctly depicted this idea when he said that a man's worth was measured by the number of children and wives he had and could feed. Today, some parents when asked why many children, will obviously answer that God gives and feed children. Some may even go to the extent of quoting the biblical verses, that God commanded man " to increase and multiply" Some Muslims would say that it is unislammic to predetermine the number of children a faithful may have, To this effect, family planning is regarded as a taboo. Dongle quotes the Newswatch magazine in Ajibola (1989) in its topic "God Gift as a problem "stated:

> *"Traditional and religious attitudes to children have always prevented rational discussion on population growth. Age-old traditional attitudes regard childbirth as an act of God, which should not be tampered with. In many Nigerian communities, children are seen as God's supreme gifts. He will always provide for them. The number of children a woman has is also a source of recognition in some communities. Mbaise in Imo state is one such community. There are special ceremonies are organized to honor a woman who has up to 10 children".*

This is predominantly among the Ibo people. It is known as " IGBU EWU UKWU". Children in such families, If they don't take proper care of, may resort to be abused. Most children from polygamous families are not properly taken care of as a result of financial background of the family. The low economic status of some

Parents may be an incentive to offenses against property of stealing on the part of some children but not a direct cause of crime. Children from homes where parents fail to satisfy their material needs and where parents are indifferent to children's progress are usually delinquent (salami 1997). The temptation to steal is greater for underprivileged children because they suffer from material deprivation and have less self control than middle group children. (Salami, 1997).

In the case of sexual abuse, family circumstances and practices constitute factors of child abuse. This occurs in some families, where there are more than five children, including the parents living in a one room apartment. There is a lack of personal privacy excessive nudity in the home, physical contact that is not entirely affectionate and an inadequate marital sexual relationship, other factors include parents allowing their underage children to watch some immoral and amorous movies in the home, all these increase the likelihood of sexual abuse on children. The influx of pornographic materials and violence on our screen at home and its resultant effect on the psyche of children, especially as depicted in some home videos produced in the country is a means of child abuse.

JUVENILE DELINQUENCY

The problems of children are as old in history as the children themselves. Juvenile delinquency has been defined by many schools of thoughts. According to Sandhu (1977) Juvenile delinquency is defined as any act; course of conduct, or situation which is referred to court for acts defined in the statutes of the states as the violation of a state law or municipal ordinance by children or youth of Juvenile court age, or for conduct so seriously antisocial as to interfere with the rights of others or to menace the welfare of the delinquent himself or of the community. This broad defection of delinquency includes conducting which violates the law only when committed by children e.g. truancy, ungovernable behavior and running away from home, indulging in sexual promiscuity, associating with criminals or other deviants, visiting places where liquor is used smoking cigarettes etc. legally speaking, the violation of state laws committed by a youth under a particular age (usually 18 and below) constitutes died infancy. The same violation committed by an adult above the age limit considered a crime.

Most of these kids involves themselves into this act as a result of influence of their peers, while some reason a result of broken homes where the come from. Some of these children are nowadays from their parents and join goings or criminals roaming about the streets pick pocking. The mingle with the crowds at very busy places, such as bus stops, markets or in rushing crowd. Some of these children when caught in the act are beating or lynched to death.

However, children behavior could lead to their abuse. For instance, a baby that is premature is likely to be more difficult to care for and more likely to be abused. Children who chronically misbehave are being-young the norm is more likely to be victims of abuse. When a child, misbehaves, there is the need to call for discipline in some cases, it may compel the parents to use a cane to discipline their children or ward. To this end, Hall (1982) asserted that when a child's actions or beliefs conflicts with the parent's view or right conduct, the child is punished forcefully. Hence there should be respect for authority, work and the preservation of order. She further stressed that a child must accept without question the parents' word on matters of right conduct.

CRASS MATERIALISM

The crazy question for material things has led to the abuse of children in our society. The "get rich quick syndrome" has eaten deep into the fabric of our society. Everybody wants to be known as a wealthy man or woman without considering the means of becoming one. Because of this syndrome, the rate of atrocities committed against children as a means of becoming rich is alarming. Children are used as an article or object of trade. This is evident in child labor, trafficking, prostitution, kidnap and demanding of huge amount of money as ransom from their parents, others kidnap and mutilate the bodies either for rituals or for other purposes.

These barbaric and wicked practices thrive because of the superstitious belief on the use of human beings for wealth and power. According to NPC/UNICEF (2001) some Nigerian believes that they can attain wealth or power through human sacrifice or the use of certain human organs notably genital organs eyes and blood for superstitious rituals. These believe have led many adults in the society to resorting to the use of children for ritual purposes. Many have been kidnapped, many beheaded while many others have had their organs mutilated and killed. Meanwhile, many innocent children have fallen victims of these barbarous crimes. For instance the incidence that led to the death of master Ikechukwu Okonkwo, who was beheaded in 1996 at Otokoto Hotel premises, which caused the uproar in the Owerri Imo State popularly known as "Otokoto scandal". This was sparked by the discovery of the severed head of eleven years old children named mentioned above, from a murderer at a police checkpoint. This, however led to the discovery of the flourishing business of child killing and sale of body parts for ritual purposes. (Thursday, 21 October 1996). Other cases abound where Ritualist are caught plucking the eyes of children, trafficking on children's heads and so on.

These barbaric practices occur as a result of crass materialism. The desperate search for wealth and the worship of the rich has misled the society into the cold embrace of evil. The 'nouveau rich' syndrome thrives as a result of the societal wrong value, where the end justified the means.

Presently, some young girls have entered into the business of being pregnant and later sold their illegitimate babies to some homes or to the highest bidder. Some sell to naturalists. It was against this backdrop that the Non-governmental organization African Network for the prevention and protection Against Child Abuse and Neglect (ANPPCAN) expressed grave concern over this illicit act of using babies as an article of trade. It noted thus:

> *There are astonishing, dis-hearting and incredible cases of child trafficking and child labour most unprecedented in this country, such as reported cases of camping of*

impregnated girls who, after delivery are paid money and dispersed without their babies whose fate none can tell, perhaps bought for ritual purpose" (Punch 1999)

In another development, Donli in Ajibola (1989) indicated that some greedy parents use their children to carry hard drugs and in some cases, make such children to swallow the drugs to beat security checks. This is sheer greed of materialism and the height of social decay. This form of abuse is contrary to the ILO conventions No 182 of 1999 according to NPN/UNICEF (2001) which targets the elimination of the 'worst forms of Child Labor"

These worst forms are defined to include all forms of slavery and practices akin to slavery, such as the sale and trafficking of children, |debt bondage and forced labor, the use, procuring or offering of a child for prostitution or for drug trafficking and which by nature or the circumstances in which it is carried put is likely to harm the health, safety or morals of children.

WAR / CRISIS

War and violent conflicts have been a veritable case of child abuse and neglect in any society. Invariably, Children are the principal victims of both types of disasters. In Nigeria, there has been a series of conflicts in various locations in the country, often sparked off by ethnic, political or religious rivalries against the background of poverty and grievances. According to NPC / UNICEF (2001) often these conflicts have taken place against a general background of poverty, fierce competition for limited resources and general frustration among youths at their lack of opportunity and poor prospects for a better life.

In some cases, politicians or elite groups are thought to have manipulated such frustration for political ends. Though, Nigeria children may not have been conscripted into soldiers, but have been engaged in some sectarian and communal conflicts. Albert in NPC / UNICEF (2001) noted that by the end of the 1990s adolescents, some in their early teens, were reported by the media to have been engaged in crimes of murder, arson and looting during clashes in several northern cities. It is obvious that during crisis, many children experience grave torture, molestation and death. The plight of children in conflict ravaged communities and towns is nonetheless grim. For instance, Aguleri - Umueleri, Ife-modakeke clashes Kano, Kaduna, Nembe, Ogoni, Ilaje and Niger Delta clashes are prominent in Nigeria. In this sense, many children have lost their parents, hence living as orphans and left to cater for themselves. In addition, the case of Ikeja bomb blast in 2002 claimed thousands of children's lives. Many lost their parents and some were missing.

In many African countries children are being conscripted into the army during the wars. Some were used in guerrilla warfare, other as spies. These untrained children are forced to the battlefield to be killed. In some cases, they are abducted by the rivalries and enslaved or detained in the prison. Game (2003) noted the Amnesty International report that children have been abducted in the street or taken from classrooms; refugee camps or camps for the internally displaced. Many others have also been taken from their homes at gunpoint as their distraught parents looked on helplessly. Others have reported being picked up while playing in their neighborhood or walking along the road.

The abduction and induction of children into wars and guerrilla armies in some of these war ravaged countries such as Liberia, Sierra Leone, Angola etc. Had been as a result of fragile and defenseless nature of children. However, while there are no reliable statistics for the number of children fighting in Africa, the problem is acute on the continent. Rebel groups in West Africa have been notorious filling their ranks with minor often by force. This has been the case with infamous Revolutionary United front is Sierra Leone and Liberians United for Reconciliation and Democracy in Liberia. The Great lakes region of Central Africa is also awash with child soldiers (Jama, 2003). Many of these children are compelled to take drugs, to numb their conscience, fear and to heighten their thrill of violence or killer instinct. In addition, it was noted that another trick of rebels in Sierra Leone was to use abducted children to attack their own villages and families. Even ten year olds, can learn to carry and use lightweight but lethal weapons, such as M16 semi- automatic rifles or the omnipresent aluminium Kalashnikov Ak 47s. It further noted that these children with no sons or daughters, wives or husbands to think of, are frequently less terrified of death than older people. In addition to this, each day, the young sierra Leonenian soldiers sang an anthem glorifying their struggle thus:

"Go and tell the president that Sierra Leone is
My home,
Go and tell my parents, they see me no more. When fighting
In the battle field I'm fighting for ever,"

From the above indication, it is obvious that African children have become increasely the casualties of modern warfare. The coalition to stop the use of child soldiers, conservatively estimates that there are 300,000 child soldiers fighting in some 40 countries across the world, with Africa nations topping the list (Jama, 2003) This shows the alarming increase in the use of child soldiers in Africa and around the globe. Furthermore, Radar Barmen, a Swedish charity in Punch(1999) indicated the statistics of soldiers thus:

Canada 200, United States 6745, Columbia 16,000 Peru 2100, Paraguay 27,700, Britain 4991 Netherlands 140, Turkey 1500, Sudan 31,000 Congo 6000+, Liberia 5000+, Angola 7000 in 1999 Uganda 5000, Burundi 10,000, Rwanda 20,000, Afghanistan 108,200.

Adequate measures need to be adopted to resolve the menace of child soldier syndrome among African Jama (2003) in his opinion to the resolution of child soldier indicated that at the end of the day, successful, stamping out of the phenomenon of child soldiers lies in identifying and properly addressing the underlying causes. Settling conflicts peacefully and ameliorating the socioeconomic situation of vulnerable communities are crucial for keeping children off the battlefields and in schools - where they belong.

CHAPTER FIVE

CONSEQUENCES OF CHILD ABUSE AND HUMAN TRAFFICKING

PSYCHO-S0CIAL CONSEQUENCES

Child abuse and neglect is a social problem that has serious social consequences. It is the child, the abusive parents, the condoning state and the society at large that reap the harvest of the ills of the abuse. The consequences are delicate and capable of running a nation. According to Donli in Ajibola (1989) the social repercussions of child abuse and neglect are frightening and are capable, if not checked, of mortgaging the future of a nation and its citizens and societal self- destruction. Hence, it is a time bomb.

It predominantly manifest in societal vices. In some broken homes, it is common to see children taken to street boys and girls. This is as a result of the crisis in the family; such as divorce, separation, death of parents, etc. These children are left without any care rather than fending for themselves. They would be out there learning some societal vices, through association with bad company. These kids would learn crimes of different forms and become criminals terrorizing the entire society. They would pay in turn, their retaliatory actions, crimes assassination, armed robbery, terrorism etc. against the society. The member of the society would be at the receiving end to feel the pinch of these crimes perpetrated by these Kids. De Goshi in its report in (Ajibola, 1989)

> Cases of armed robbery, theft and violence by our youths are daily on the increase... It is no longer a pride or pleasure to ride in a brand new & flashy car. Chances are, the driver would lose his life and his car to come young hoodlums. Electronic gadgets are no longer safe in our heavily barricaded homes. Young, healthy criminals go in gangs of tens depriving owners of the gadgets. Nighttime that is suppose to be a time for repose and rest becomes a time of toil and dread.

The society thus lives in constant fear of these young men who have decided to threaten the whole society. In Lagos state, for example many children have their abode under bridges. These kids are delinquent and involved in many crimes ranging from pick pocketing smuggling, stealing to robbery. Some of them commit these crimes under the influence of drugs.

Consequently, the female children that are exposed early to the society through hawking are impregnated by adults. It is obvious that these inexperienced young girls are easily lured by men into doing what they may never have thought of or even ought to know. The result normally becomes pregnant.

TEENAGE PREGNANCY

Teenage pregnancy sometimes called "mistaken pregnancy" has been on the increase in the country over the years. In some cultures and tradition, it is a taboo and shameful act for a teenage girl to be pregnant. More so, when she gets the pregnancy out of wedlock. Naturally, every female child is looked upon as a pride of her family. If she keeps herself and remains a virgin before her marriage, she is recommended and respected in her family. On the other hand, if she abuses this virtue, she is considered a spoilt and wayward child. If by chance, a female child gets pregnant, the family usually sends her away to another place to stay rather than her home because the society would simply conclude that they did not train her well.

Nowadays, teenage pregnancy has become a pride. Teenagers get pregnant and carry it with pride. Wehweh (2000) asserted "these days, that which used to bring shame to the family, has become the in-thing in our society. These days the rate at which teenage girls get pregnant calls for concern. However to think that this no longer brings shame to them makes matters worse. Parents send their daughters to school with the expectation that the latter would bring back the good results of academic achievement instead; she comes back with pregnancy and does not feel remorse about the whole thing. Indeed, she rather carries it about with pride. And what next? The girl drops out of school in order to look after her child. While her mates are at school, she is busy looking after a child".

The act is also rampant among female girls sent out hawking on the street. They usually get impregnated by blokes irresponsible men on the streets. Many cases of such abound in the society. A teenage girl who gets pregnant has been deprived of the joy of her teenage life. Hence, she is saddled with adult responsibilities. She would be regarded as second-hand or tokunbo. Her chances of getting married are narrow. In some cases, during childbirth these teenagers have serious medical problems. One among the diseases associated with teenagers during childbirth is a Vesico Vaginal Fistula (VVF). In elucidating this vividly, Fayoyin (1993) in his report on "The menace of VVF in Nigeria" narrated the story of a girl thus:

> *"Grace, a primary school pupil in ikot Ekpene Akwa Ibom State became pregnant at 11years. Due to ignorance and shame, she hid her pregnancy from her guardian until it was too late for any remedial action. Throughout her pregnancy, she did not have any form of antenatal care,*

during her labor which lasted for two weeks, long enough to feature in the Guinness Book of World Records, she was transferred back and forth traditional birth attendants native doctors and the church. Somehow, her guardians "forget" that maternity clinics are established for such purpose. When all else failed, she was delivered of a dead, decomposed baby through a gruesome traditional "surgery" of forcing a long stick through her mouth to her abdomen, which bloated her and forcefully expelled the baby. This resulted in multiple arterial rupture and VVF, Vestico, Vaginal, Fistula. It took about 20 repair operations spread over four years to rehabilitate her. Grace may never have a husband or a baby".

This callous disruption in the life of a growing female child ultimately affects the society. The impact is not usually felt at the point of conception, but much later when the girl becomes a nursing mother and eventually ends up being a liability to the family and by extension the rest of the society.

ILLITERACY

Illiteracy is another psychosocial consequences of child abuse. Any child is that denied education couldn't read or write, hence he or she is termed an illiterate. Therefore, illiteracy is a disease which only education can cure. It dwindles the nation, politically, socially and economically. However, many developing countries neglect the early childhood dedication "According to Odudu (1999) cited carol Bellarny thus:

> *" The illiteracy rate in developing countries may triple to the billion mark in the next century if governments in such countries do not take immediate steps to engender early childhood education".*

The grim picture of education in developing countries as contained in the 1999 state of the world's children report by UNICEF lames the unfortunate situation on the reluctance of many governments to enforce the 1989 convention on the right of the child (Odudu,1999) illiteracy is a bane to the development of any society. Hence it makes it hard for people to interact in a spirit of understanding, harmony, peace and gender equality among all people. It is obvious that without proper education people cannot work productively to promote the economic condition of the society, care for health, sustain and promote themselves, and more so live culturally enriched lives.

The growth of any nation depends mostly on the level of educational attainment of the citizenry. This must start from childhood. Education provides people with knowledge and skills, which are vital for a national growth .Children who are denied of this opportunity, are considered abuse and neglected.

There has been an increase in school dropouts and low school intake in the country as a result of parental Ignorance and deliberate decision to abuse and neglect the children.

Poverty has been identified as a prevailing factor in the denial of childhood education. Poverty constituted 85% of the high rate of illiteracy in Nigeria. Children drop out of school to help the family need to make ends meet, while some are withdrawn on the basis that their parents cannot pay their school fees and are forced to work.

Callaway's (1981) supporting this fact while outlining the causes of the drop out of children from school remarked that:

"The likelihood of children being withdrawn from school to take part in productive activities at home is increased in a situation where those who do complete school are unable to find satisfactory employment.

Investment in education, then becomes a more doubtful proportion, especially for poor families. Growing unemployment among school leavers in Nigeria not only among primary school leavers but secondary school leavers too, may thus aggravate the dropout problem".

He further stated that sometime girls in upper primary classes or secondary schools are withdrawn to be married occasionally they become pregnant and are forced to leave school. Ill-health, perhaps combined with under-nourishment may be of greater consequences in some rest than in others.

Even if children are formally enrolled, they may be pulled out of school to assist farming activities during peak periods of the agricultural year. In some parts of the country, children's involvement in cattle herding or fishing has similar consequences. For example, a study in three riverine areas of the south - south zone (Bonny/Ardoni Brass / Kalabari and segbama / Yenagoa) found that 76 percent of children aged 6-16 were not attending school, either because of the difficulties of access to schools or the involvement of children in fishing (Ezewu and Tahir, 1997).

However the 1989 convention on the rights of the child, which has been ratified by almost all countries in the world stipulates Articles 28 and 29, that countries should provide free compulsory basic schooling that is aimed at developing each child's ability to the fullest (Odudu,1999). Nigeria as a country is not exempted yet unfortunately in most rural and urban areas, it is common to come across underage children hawking along the streets when they are supposed to be in the classroom learning.

Some other factors that contributed to this, are frustrating nature of the educational system, lack of parental supervision and assistance, lack of facilities in school, lack of books and teaching aids, excessive and unwarranted corporal punishment and finally sexual harassment by teachers.

There is consensus that child care and early education are inseparable, children cannot be well cared for without being educated and children cannot be well educated without being cared for (odudu'1999).

Vi's-à-is this Okafor (1981) stressed that the most important period of man's education is that of the early years of his development when the mind is most tender and pliable it is of prime importance to see that the combination of circumstance and conditions which surrounds the child during this period of his formation is as very close to the ideal as possible. He further stated that the child's early education would be more effective, lasting if it is received in a well-ordered and well-disciplined family. The government, however, should put more effort in enhancing early childhood education by the provision of free basic education is the right of the child and ensure the effectiveness of the Universal Basic Education program in Nigeria.

In the urban areas, it is common to see a boy under the age of 13 - 15 exposed to hackney business (conductor). It is at this level that future robbers are a breed which the media grandstand them as kid robbers.

If a child at this age start having access to money and start doing what the drivers are doing. He may grow up thinking that all there is to life is money, tobacco, drink and street girls. This child is ultimately a time bomb, leaving the society in the fear of explosion.

On the issue of human trafficking, however, the levels of causality, physical brutality and psychological trauma suffered by slaves in the 19th Century were probably significantly higher than levels endured to prevailing standards of welfare, health, and societal expectations, the physical and mental pain sustained by today's slave victims of human trafficking is probably at least as much as those in earlier times. Some of today's 'slaves' are subjected to abuse and humiliation that are as shocking as anything recorded from the early centuries. Children are beaten daily tortured, fed on cat food and forbidden to leave the confines of their work space. Some endure sexual abuse by pedophiles owners and their friends (Obadina, 2001:28).

Nigerians have been highly devalued and looked down on by foreigners. This has brought about the victim syndrome. Trafficking has a lot of debilitating effects on the individual. Victims are susceptible to various diseases such as syphilis, gonorrhea and even HIV/AIDS. They also tend to age more rapidly due to strenuous work involved.

In the society, they are held in disdain and called unprintable names and are wrapped in eternal social stigma. Due to the low-self esteem of the Nigerian women, the foreigners value them less. Given the less value attached to Nigerian women, they are lured or forced to have sex with dogs and gorillas in front of the cameras. Presently, Nigerian trafficked girls are used for experimenting on fertilization and reproduction with ages and dogs to test whether the eggs of humans and the sperms of animals can produce a viable offspring.

Consequently, those victims who are repatriated or deported have problem of reintegration into the Society. Thus, they have lost the sense of self-confidence and self-reliance.

POLITICAL CONSEQUENCES

The future of any nation depends on the well being of their children, hence they saying "children re the future of tomorrow". Besides, if these children are abused and neglected, they will be ill-prepared youths. These youths who are suppose to be future leaders only engage in the politics of treachery and calumny, which can only lead to maladjustive insensitive and sadistic adults in the future.

Children born in a crime, conflict and war infested areas are bound psychological to grow with negative ideologies. This is obvious where children are suspended under psychological holocaust with sophisticated war arsenals spread all over their country and forcefully conscripted into the armies and guerrilla warfare's. These children would grow up only to think that crime, war and conflict are all in life. When placed in a position where they will make policy decisions such a child would not hesitate to lead his society through violence.

According to punch (1999) children who had no training or education beyond the use of a gun or a rocket propelled grenade are harder to demobilize and bring back into routine life than grown-up fighters, In the similar vein Mr. Otunnu in his interview opined that group that recruit child soldiers tend to find themselves with a big problem when peace comes or even when it does not. They find a generation of children carrying guns who knows only the gun culture who hang around on street everywhere with guns "(punch, 1999).

"Good reputation is better than riches," they say. Traffickers who trafficked and smuggle children out of this country either for prostitution or other purposes are not doing good for the image of Nigeria. These girls when smuggled out of Europe, throws courtesy to the wind and behaves animalistic and the image of the country is dented. Hence Nigerians in the international scene are regarded as notorious in prostitution.

On the issue of human trafficking, the impact on the political image of Nigeria cannot be over emphasized. According to Edo State Governor, Chief Lucky Igbinedion, the ugly trade had done great damage to the image of the State (Edo) and Nigeria" (Dialogue, April 2004:15).

The problem of human trafficking led to a diplomatic face off between Nigeria and Benin Republic. In early August, 2003, Nigeria's President Obasanjo closed the border with Benin in Protest at the Benin Government's lack of cooperation in tackling problems such as people (human) trafficking. Although, the border was reopened a week later following a summit between Obasanjo and Benin's President Mathew Kerekou at which the Nigerian leader extracted pledges of strong cooperation (Africa Today, November 2003:16).

The civilized world sees Nigeria as a country where anything goes, a country of cannibals; a country where the dignity of man and morality is never respected; a country which does not recognize the citizenry, a country where containers carry human beings and not goods; a country where trade in human beings remains a brisk business and in welcome development, a country where crime no longer shocks anybody.

Besides, human trafficking exposes Nigeria as a huge nation of disappointments, where poverty reigns supreme and is used as an excuse for sordid or illegalities. Thus, many countries have tightened their diplomatic noose against Nigeria. Whenever it comes to Nigeria, most Western Countries apply stringent immigration laws. Sometimes Nigerians are humiliated at the entry points of these countries as they are thoroughly searched before allowing them entry.

ECONOMIC CONSEQUENCES

According to Donli in Ajibola (1989) Child abuse has both negative and positive economic consequences. The negative side is the premature incorporation of the child into the labor force. This is the child exploitative work, which hinders or hampers his normal physical, mental, social and psychological development for meaningful adult life. The child though working is not adequately paid for his wages. He is subjected to tedious and hazardous working environment for long hours and therefore suffer from exhaustion and over work. He is stunted physically and intellectually that hinders him from acquiring the basic education necessary for his mental development. Some of these children take the responsibility of the parents / guardians by shouldering the heavy financial burden of catering for this unemployed, poor parents.

These children have been denied education hence lacks skills, and the nation is robbed of manpower requirement in the future.

In the positive side, Donli (1989) attributed this to the massive contribution of child labour to the economy. He further stressed that this can be seen from the sheer number of figures of children in Africa under the age of 13 engaged in child labor at 16 million, while the figure supplied by the international labor organization, for children in Africa under the age of 15, engages in regular employment is about 10 million.

In relation to this, the cost of employing adult would be reduced to minimal because they are ready to take any amount given to them by their employer. Employers take advantage of these children. Thus the children are used and exploited.

Due to economic situation of the country, most children are subjected to labour. They do this, to assist the family in their financial needs. These children by so doing are denied education. Once a child is denied education, he is handicapped in life. He grows up to become less productive. Hence the level of manpower development is intimately reduced, thereby denied the country the manpower growth. The effect of denying a child his/ her educational right has contributed to the vicious circle of poverty. This is evident in the use of children by their parents as mendicants on the streets. These children are sometimes seen along the streets carried under the scorching sun and pathetically displayed by their losing mothers to attract public sympathy culminating in financial assistance, these children becomes parasite to the society and the society bears the pinches of these unproductive children in one-way or the other.

ECONOMIC IMPACT

On the issue of Human Trafficking, economically speaking, several African victims of trafficking have drowned in the Mediterranean sea and others in trouble in their futile attempt to reach Spain or Italy. Some of the child victims are used for rituals, organ transplant and other forms of economic exploitation.

The economic implication is this, while the sending countries have their human resources / work force depleted the receiving / host country are busy exploiting the cheap labor (which they pay little or nothing) for their economic advancement because these trafficked slaves generates surplus value that is not adequately compensated. A Country or Continent that continues to lose its most active human resources is set to blurring its chances of economic and technological growth. The traffickers on their part become a class of unproductive Africans that would have industrialized African Nations, but are now parasitic ring of money launderers.

The victims become suppressed; marginalized, traumatized in the plantations and because of these, acquire an altered mindset which discourages imagination, productivity, ingenuity and enterprise.

Other Countries see African Countries as insecure therefore, are not ready to risk their investment. By so doing, Africa continues to lose foreign direct investments.

HEALTH

Death and diseases are the dual evil associate to abuse and neglect of children. Children are raped battered and neglected medically and the result in death. Cases of children dying every day on our highways who were sent hawking by their parents/guardian are many. The female children sent hawking sometimes came back impregnated by the older blokes and left without care, which may eventual lead to their death. Those forced into international prostitution by their parents or the adults usually return with deadly diseases that defies every medical attention. On the other hand may spread the disease and if not properly controlled may ruin the entire society.

Consequently, in some rural areas where health facilities are almost non-existent children in such places die easily from preventable childhood killer diseases. The group of armies of lame and cripple children today is as a result of medical neglect by their parents and adults. Most of these children are prone to diseases because of malnutrition, lack of good pipe borne water and other basic social amenities.

During wars and crisis children rated the highest death toll. Many died of malnutrition such as kwashiorkor and other related diseases. Many are abandoned and later died as a result of starvation and diseases.

AFRICAN CHILD AND AIDS SCOURGE

AIDS is a disease that has claimed thousands of lives in the African continent and else where children are the worst hit of this scourge. Children are the overwhelming majority of those who live in poverty, and killer diseases, such as HIV/AIDS in Africa.

Most children have lost their parents due to this scourge, hence many have been left without care. These children orphaned by AIDS scourge are stigmatized by the society and are avoided.

Research revealed that AIDS in Africa has orphaned many children than anywhere else in the world. Of the many vulnerable members of the society, children who lost one or both parents are among the most expose of all the orphaned run greater risk of malnourished and stunted growth. These children are denied educational opportunities and many of them are left to their fate. Some are used as object of economic value or left to fend for themselves, which exposes them to all manners of social vices. This is particularly true in sub-Sahara Africa, where few social services are largely inadequate. In Nigeria the number of children scourged by human immunodeficiency virus /acquired immune deficiency syndrome (HIV/AIDS) epidemic has been put at 1.3m in 2005. According to Rita Akpan, a former Woman Affairs Minister who indicated this, noted that this is as a result of a number of orphans which continue to rise in the years ahead due to the large number of adults already living with the virus. She estimated that over 11million children under the age of 15 living in Sub-Sahara Africa has been robbed of one or both parents with HIV/AIDS (Guardian June 16 2005)

Olaoye (1999) stated that the National budgets are strained by the demands of this situation. By 2005, the health sector costs for HIV /AIDS are expected to account for more than a third of the government health- spending in Ethiopia, more than half in Kenya and nearly two thirds in Zimbabwe. He further stressed that a study in Zambia for example, showed that 32 percent of orphans in urban areas were not enrolled in school, as compared with 25% in children with parents.

Children who have been orphaned by AIDS may not also receive the health care they need, and sometimes this is because it is assumed they are inflicted with HIV and their illness are untreatable. Increasely, children whose parents are dead accumulate greater burdens of responsibility as heads of household. Often emotionally vulnerable and financially desperate, orphaned children are most likely to be sexually abused and forced into exploitative situations such as prostitution and other forms of child abuse, as a means of survival.

What then is the place of the child in an African perspective?

Children in this part of the world are said to suffer the worst form of dehumanization.

CHAPTER SIX

THE MULTIDIMENSIONAL INDICES FOR THE RESOLUTION OF CHILD ABUSE AND HUMAN TRAFFICKING IN NIGERIA - AFRICA

LEGAL ENFORCEMENT OF BASIC RIGHTS OF THE CHILD

Every human being has the fundamental right to live. Human rights are inherent in man; they arise from the very nature of man as a social animal. They are those rights which all human beings enjoy by virtue of their humanity, whether black, white, yellow, Malay, or red, the deprivation of which would constitute a grave affront to one's natural sense of justice (Ajomo, 1993). The fundamental human rights include the right to life; right to the dignity of the human person; the right to personal liberty; right to freedom of expression etc.

According to chapter 4 sections 33 to 46 of the constitution of the federal Rep. Of Nigeria 1999 section 33(1) provides: "Every person has a right to life and no one shall be deprived intentionally of his life, save in execution of the sentence of a court on respect of a criminal offense of which he has been found guilty in Nigeria" (C.R.P, 1999).Also in section 34(1) provides:

"Every individual is entitled to respect for the dignity of his person ad according

(a) No person shall be subjected to fortune or regarding treatment.

(b) No person shall be held in slavery or servitude; and

(c) No person shall be required to perform forced or compulsory labor" (CRP, 1999).

The fundamental rights stated above are the constitutional framework that guards individual or person within the Nigeria jurisdiction. However, they are not to be enjoyed in semantics only or in their mere inclusion in the pages of the constitution, but to be interpreted and executed appropriately children are not in exception of these rights, hence they are human beings. Therefore, what seem good for the goose is also good for the gander. They should be given their rights. Discrimination, neglect and abuse of children are against the principles of fundamental human right. The children in an untold number have been neglected discriminated and abuse in different manners, hence their fundamental human rights are violated. Many have been deprived of their rights. Suffice it to say, that it is an offense for a person with custody of a child under sixteen to abuse and neglect the child in a manner likely to cause him unnecessary suffering or injury to health and failure to provide adequate food, clothing, medical aid or lading for the child or to take steps to procure them are deemed to constitute neglect (Eckelaar, 1978). Various specific offenses have been created, such as permitting children to be in brothel allowing them to be used for begging, abduction, kidnaping, forced labour, trafficking, sexual abuse and prostitution, abandon etc.

Meanwhile, in the case of protection of children, many movements and organizations had called for the enactment of Bills of rights for children. The royal commission on family and children's law in British Columbia (1975) (Berger Commission) gave three reasons for seeking such a measure. First, it would put in positive from matters that are presently approached in a negative fashion (the threat to remove a child if neglected could be seen as a right of the child not to be neglected). Secondly, it would encourage the recognition of individual capacities and identities of children in court proceedings. Third, it would introduce the dimension of the child's point of view in decisions affect their interests.

The commission proceeding is identified twelve children's right's, including the right to an environment free from 'physical abuse, exploitation and degrading treatment'. The Berger commission goes as far as to suggest that a child whose rights are violated should have a remedy by way of 'judicial declaration' of entitlement to the right, which, it would be hoped, would not be ignored by the state authorities (Eekelaar, 1978). It is possible that enactment of a code of this nature might provide a stimulus to state action. It is also possible that it might provide a framework within which lawyers could bring about an improvement in the lives of some children.

According to Eekelaar (1978), the major concern of these movements seems to be the encouragement of an attitude towards children, which sees them not in terms of objects for the fulfillment of the needs of adults but as individuals in their own right. Suggesting that it becomes the duty of society to ensure that the interest of each individual child is to be safeguarded, during its childhood, then the child will be in a position to maximize its inherent capabilities on reaching maturity. This is not to be assumed that it implies the removal of all restrictions on a child during, its development (Eekelaar1978).

Sharp (1970) indicated that there was also the declaration in Geneva of the rights of the child "by the Convention which was signed by all members of the fifth General council of the save the children international union on Feb 28th 1924 presented and adopted by the Fifth Assembly of the league of nations on Sept 26th 1924. It reads thus:

"By the present declaration of the rights of the child, commonly known as the "Declaration of Geneva "the men and women of all nations, recognized that as their duty that, beyond and above all considerations of race, nationality or creed.

1. THE CHILD must be given the means requisite for its normal development, both mentally, and spiritually.
2. THE CHILD that is hungry must be fed, the child that is sick must be nursed, the child that is backward must be helped, the delinquent child must be reclaimed, and the orphan and the wait must be sheltered and succored.
3. THE CHILD must be the first to receive relief in times of distress.

4. THE CHILD must be put in a position to earn a livable hood and must be protected against every form of exploitation.
5. THE CHILD must be brought into the consciousness that its talents must be devoted to the service of its fellow men (Sharp, 1970).

In addition, it was in recognition of the importance of children and the need for their survival that the UNITED NATION General Assembly adopted in 1989 a Declaration on the Rights of the children (Ahiante, 2000).

Notwithstanding, in November 1989, the general Assembly of UN adopted the convention on children's rights, which was followed by the summit meeting on children, committing the participating countries to a program for the protection of children's rights and for their lives. The convention on children's rights establishes the Right of Children to grow up, to be protected and cared for, and right to development and participation in the convention bans child labor, child prostitution, protects refugee children gives homeless children the right to health care and basic education (Ahiante, 2000).

Many children have been denied their basic rights because of their defenseless nature. Naturally, a child has the right to life. According to Okeke, the child has the right in survival. This implies that the child has to be provided the wherewithal to live as comfortable as possible. He should be provided adequate training to both at home and in school to enable him to cope with the going-on in the society and get better equipped for more productive adult life. The child has to be protected and fortified to grapple with the societal influence. In other words, he should be provided with such experiences and enriching background to enable him to cope with the vagaries of the society. He has to be guided and respected. Both by parents and adult members of the society to enable him to acquire knowledge, understanding and perform his role in the society, for the present and in the future.

He has to be protected from self-abuse arising from Ignorance, deprivation or neglect. He has right to adequate education, medical attention good nurture and protection from hazards. Thus, children should not be exposed to dangers and conditions that would constitute a threat to their existence and progress. The child should be provided such opportunities that could lead to the maximum activation and attainment of his potentials (Okeke, 2003).

According to Ogbeh (2001) In the UN, convention for the Rights of the child, children's rights are categorically stated as rights to: surviving. Development and participation, but basic principles of children's right are:

* Every child has the right to live and be allowed to assemble according to the Law.
* Every child has the right to express opinions and free communication on any issue subject to restriction under the law.

* Every child is entitle to protection from any act that interferes with his or her civi l honour, compulsory basic education depending on individual ability.
* Every child is entitled to good health, protection from illness and proper medical attention for survival, personal growth and development.
* Every child must be protected from indecent and inhuman treatment through sexual exploitation child labour, torture, maltreatment and neglect.
* No child should suffer any discrimination perspective of ethnic origin, birth, color, sex, language, religion, political beliefs, status or disability.

The Nigerian government in their effort to join the UN's program for the protection of children's rights, have put in several reforms which include:

(a) The Nigeria Labor Act of 1990 which protects the child from exploitation and abuse

(b) The Cinematography Act of 1990, which protects the child from exposure to indecent and obscene materials, publications and films.

(c) The Tobacco and Alcohol Advertisement Decrees, which forbids the use of children in the advertisement of cigarette and alcohol beverages.

(d) The children and young person lows of 1958.

(e) The criminal laws which prohibit the sale and trafficking of children

(f) A draft of children's Degree, which took into consideration the UN Convention on the Rights of the Child.

(g) The OAU Chapters on the Rights and Welfare of the child (Ahiante, 2000).

With these reforms and the declaration of the Rights of the child by the UN, it still leaves children at the mercy of their parents, as the persons who are entrusted to seek for their children's best interest. The declaration of the rights of the child was the initiatives of the UN to promote the child's happiness, enjoyment for its own good and for the good of the society. It is a clarion call upon parents, men and women as individuals, voluntary organizations, local authorities and national governments to recognize their rights and strive for the observance by legislative and other good measures taken in accordance with the above principles.

THE LEGITIMACY OF NAPTIP IN THE CONTROL/PREVENTION OF HUMAN TRAFFICKING IN NIGERIA.

Piqued by the odious and threatening practices of the evil of human trafficking and child labour, wreaking havoc on human lives and image dainting within Nigeria and beyond, the Trafficking in persons (prohibition) law Enforcement and Administration Act No 24 enacted by the National Assembly of the Federal Republic of Nigeria signed into law on July 14, 2003, established corporate Agency body to be known as the National Agency for prohibition of traffic in persons and other related matters on August 8, 2003, and vested it with the responsibility to enforce laws against Traffic in persons, investigation and prosecute persons suspected to be engaged in traffic in persons, and to take charge and co-ordinate the rehabilitation and counseling of Trafficked persons, and for related matters.

The Agency is a body corporate with perpetual succession and has a common seal. The Agency is empowered among others to enforce the due administration of the Act as well as adopting measures to increase the effectiveness of eradication of traffic in persons.

Furthermore, the Agency is responsible for enhance the effectiveness law enforcement agents to suppress traffic in persons; taking such measures and or in collaboration with other agencies or bodies that may ensure the elimination and prevention of the root causes of the problem of traffic in any person, strengthening and enhancing effective legal means for international co-operation in criminal matters for suppressing the international activities of traffic in persons; taking charge, supervising, controlling and co-ordinating the rehabilitation of trafficked persons and participating in proceedings relating to traffic in persons.

Other provisions of the Act, according to NAPTIP News (2005/06) indicated thus:

Any person who procures, uses or offers any other person for prostitution, or the production of pornography, or for pornographic performance; and any person who traffics any other for the purpose of forced or compulsory recruitment use in armed conflict, commits an offense and is liable on conviction to imprisonment for fourteen years without an option or fine.

It also provides that any person who conspires with another to induce any person under the age of eighteen years by means of any false pretense or other fraudulent means, permits any man to have unlawful carnal knowledge of such person commits an offense and is liable on conviction to imprisonment for five years, among others.

The Agency is headed by an Executive Secretary. There are four specialized units, namely investigation, legal and prosecution, public Enlightenment, and counseling and Rehabilitation.

PSYCHO-SOCIAL AND ECONOMIC APPROACH

In an attempt to resolve the crisis of child abuse and human trafficking in Africa, in the past, efforts have been geared towards selective approach. One or two approaches have been isolated and implemented as a way or ways of tackling this social anathema whereas the problem of child abuse continues to loom and the business of human trafficking continues to boom.

Considering the fact that this problem have eaten deep into the fabrics of our society, it calls for concerted sustainable and multimedia efforts to clamp down on these obnoxious and most criminal atrocity. It should not be mono-sectoral or mono-organizational neither should it be left in the hands of the victims to exact compensation or remedial actions from their exploiters. The issue of abuse and trafficking should be the concern of all; it should not be left as a private non-government human right issue. The government, the non-governmental organizations, all sectors must be involved.

Nonetheless, the following panacea is proffered which has a far reaching and multi –faceted approach to the eradication of human trafficking as a form of abuse.

(a) Creation of alternative source of income in the countries of departure. This approach is premised on the assumption that the prompting force for trafficking is economic. Skill acquisition and provision of financial services if creatively applied could be very effective.

(b) Creation of vocational centers for skills acquisition after which the victims could work and for themselves as well as assist family members. This will encourage self-reliance of the young men and women. In this case, the activities of the Edo child trust fund and Idia Renaissance is worthy of commendation. The trust fund has trained more 900 young girls in the state – Lift Above Poverty Organization have been assisting the young girls who graduated from the skills acquisition center with micro credit loans to start a small scale business and credit loans to start small scale business and with the active support of Edo state government.

(c) Enlightenment campaigns: there should be more awareness campaigns through information dissemination on the evil of trafficking in women and children abroad for forced prostitution and other illicit gains. This enlightenment should be extended to schools, market places, vocation centers and motor parks. Seminars and workshops should be organized to educate and equally train social workers who would need to go to the rural areas to educate people not give their word to people who may involve them in forced prostitution abroad and other forms of child. Labor and illicit trade in human beings. It is here too, that the activities of Women Trafficking and Child Labor Eradication Foundation (WOTCLEF) are commendable. The pioneering efforts of the leader/founder of WOTCLEF, Hajia Titi Amina Abubakar has brought the issue of human trafficking to the front burner through Radio/ television programs in particular, the popular national network program on the Nigeria television Authority half – hour soap operation titled Izozo, televised every Tuesday between 8.00 – 830pm. This has created much awareness to the ignorant, the deceived and the hoodwinked to the evils of human trafficking. In the recent time, the commitment of Hajia Titi Abubakar's led WOTCLF has found expression in the recent apprehensions of various trafficking syndicates and their bulk of human Cargoes – across the length and breadth of Nigeria. More so, now, the activities of WOTCLEF has led to the passage of anti – trafficking. Bills/laws at the National Assembly and some state houses of Assembly, including Edo, Anambra and Cross Rivers States aimed at suppressing the illicit activity (Olaniyi 2004:65). Besides, some states such as the Kano State Government has also undertaken tough measures. The police in that State recently nabbed suspected human trafficking with 19 persons who were being prepared for "export" to Europe en – route Libya (Dialogue, April 2004:5).

(b) Stigmatization of the act trafficking in stronger words by the society. Until there is a social stigma attached to human trafficking, the perpetrators would continue. Some parents support their daughters and perpetrators with prayers and charms to protect them. But social stigma would discourage the practice of people taking pride in sending their children abroad for prostitution.

(c) De – emphasizing crass materialism through reorientation. People should be reoriented that they should not give much value to material things at the expense of their children's welfare.

(d) Religious/traditional Approach: churches should come out strongly against the act. Also, there should be revival of age – old traditional custom, traditional ethics of declaring openly that evil money should not be respected. It was a thing of pride for a young girl in African traditional to remain a virgin till she married. This value has been relegated to the background in the society, and should be re –inculcated into our young females.

(e) Effective involvement of traditional institutions: our traditional rulers, chiefs, kings and their councils should be inculcated in the anti – human trafficking. For example, in Benin, the Oba of Benin, Omo 'N' Oba Nedo, Uku Akpoloppolor and his chiefs should be involved in the fight against human trafficking. A battle waged by the palace through the chiefs and Enigies is capable of confronting the problem. (Dialogue April 2004:6)

(f) The social Revolutionary Approach: The struggle against international trafficking and prostitution in Nigeria, can also come genuinely from the mass of the oppressed people of this country. The struggle should be linked with the entire struggle against the continuous imperialist exploitation of Nigeria.

In the light of above, there is a proliferation of NGO's engaged in anti-human trafficking campaigns. The include Idia Renaissance, International organization on migration based in Europe, International Reproductive right research action group (IRRAG); Girls power initiative (GPI), life above poverty organization (LAPO), African women Empowerment group (AWEG), committee for the support of the dignity of women (ASUDOW), Alliances for Africa (AFA), Women in Nigeria (Win) and the host of others involved in collaborative work to put an end to the malaise in the country.

Apart from the above, the recent nationwide seminars and workshops have been organized by WOTCLEF led by its indefatigable leader – Hajia Amina Titi Abubakar. This is an eloquent testimony of her effort to restore the dignity and morality of women in particular and children in general.

SERVICE DELIVERY PROGRAMMES FOR VICTIMS

There is a need for service programs for victims of child abuse and the victims of human trafficking in the society. Positive responses to the needs of victims of crime such as child abuse and human trafficking in the society could lead to the approval and enactment of appropriate legislation that would give legal backing to the establishment of the service delivery programs as is the case in most of the developed nations.

According to Odoemenam (199), Effort like that had resulted in the child Abuse prevention and treatment Act (PL 93-247) that was signed into law in January 1974. The Act had established a National Centre on Child Abuse and Neglect in the Children's Bureau Office of Child Development, United State Department of health, Education Welfare. In all victim service programs, the dominant theme has to be a recovery, which may be a short or long term and deal with problems that are physical, emotional, and financial or the combination of the three. He further stressed that victims service progremmes could be divided into primary, secondary and tertiary functions primary function's common to most programmes are immediate in nature and are aimed at delivering narrow range of direct service like taking immediate responsibility for the victim is provided with emergency medical or social services, providing the victim with a temporary companion, addressing the victim's family needs, ensuring that further exploitation of the victim does not occur following up on delivery of public assistance to clients (Odoemenam, 1994).

Secondary function he said are also common to most programmes but are usually of lesser importance, have long -range systems, impacts and are broad in scope some secondary functions include helping victims in their roles as witnesses, providing advice to reduce the victims risk of revictimzation establishing volunteer efforts of augment victims service units, rendering to victims and their families with aftermath arrangement such as funerals insurance and victims compensation among many other functions.

From the above ideas, the introduction and establishment at victims of child abuse and human trafficking service programme will go a long way in reducing physical impact, sense of loss and degradation, embarrassment and humiliation mental trammel and psychological effects which victim suffer. Finally it will give the victims sense of belonging in the society, since it would come out clear to them when they benefit from such programme, that their fellow citizens, governments. and religions organizations and other agencies have cared and shared in their misfortunes.

EFFECTIVE DISCIPLINE TO A CHILD

Many parents are yet to know the effective ways of disciplining their children. Lack of knowledge of these has led many people into abuse and children. Discipline is the method of training both the mind and the body to produce obedience and self-control. Child psychologist Marcial Lasswell provides many practical guidelines for parents who want their disciple to be both effective and humane. Underlying all of the guideline, however, is the basic notion that all parents should become informed about child development so that they know what to expect of children at certain ages. Many children most of the time want to be good and to please their parents. Much of the behavior that the parent sees as problems may result from the child's lack of experience and poor judgment.

Lasswell (1987) suggested thus:

1. Parents should make clear rules that are consistently enforced. The reason behind rules can be explained to children as soon as they can understand. Having fever rules, consistently enforced works better than having many rules frequently broken.
2. When a child appears to be misbehaving, parents should find out what really happened before jumping to conclusion.
3. Never punish a child for feelings, only for actions. A child has a right to his or her feeling, but how they are expressed many need guidance. "I feel like writing you" can be met with "why are so angry" "I am going to hit

you" can lead to a discussion of the consequences of such behaviour and on exploration of better ways to handle anger. If, however, a child does hit a parent, the action calls for discipline (unless the parent wishes to encourage hitting).

4. The timing of intervention following misbehaviour can be critical. The time Interval between the act and the intervention, particularly with young children the less effective the parent will be in changing the child's behavior. However, old children sometimes find the waiting period while parents decide on a punishment worse than the punishment itself

5. The simplest way to eliminate negative behavior is to be certain that there are no rewards attached to it. It is rare that any behavior continues unless it is somehow reinforced. Of course, parents are not always about to eliminate rewards (such as attention from friends or the perverse pleasure some children gain from riling their parents). In such cases, rewarding behavior. Parents want to encourage, can work nearly as well.

6. Parents should refrain from intervening if they fell out of control. Allow a cooling-off period that is long enough to restore calm but not so long as to render the intervention unsuccessful. "Time out" (by sending a child from the room; to example) can help both parents and children calm down.

7. Parents should learn how to accommodate their children's behavior. A home in which there is positive support, love and security are more effective for sharing children's character than any one style of discipline.

According to Baumrind (1977) discipline does not need to be harsh to be effective.From a review of the research on punishment, the following facts emerge:

1. Punishment is most effective when it is closely associated in time with the undesired behavior.
2. Punishment should be accompanied by an explanation of why the behavior was wrong, and alternate behavior should be offered so that child can be redirected
3. The punishment should "fit the crime" as much as possible so that the child makes an association between the act and the punishment.

Hall (1982) asserted that parents now expect achievements of their children, rewarding their successes and punishing their failures, are likely to have children with a strong urge to succeed. Children's attitude toward their successes or failures depend upon the causes to which they cannot control, they may simply give up a condition called learned helplessness.

CHAPTER SEVEN

THE MODELS OF PRO-ACTIVE CRUSADE AGAINST CHILD ABUSE AND HUMAN TRAFFICKING IN NIGERIA

NATIONAL AGENCY FOR THE PROHIBITION OF TRAFFIC IN PERSONS AND OTHER RELATED MATTERS (NAPTIP): A ROLE MODEL IN AFRICA.

In a bid to restore the dignity of man, control and prevent the modern day slavery known as human trafficking and child labor, the Obasanjo Administration via the trafficking in persons (prohibition) law Enforcement and Administration Act 2003, established an administrative structure and entity known as the National Agency for prohibition of traffic in persons and other Related matters (NAPTIP). This anti-trafficking in persons law is a comprehensive piece of legislation aimed at fighting trafficking in persons and other allied offense (both internal and external trafficking) in all its ramifications.

The Agency is empowered among others, to enforce the due administration of the Act as well as coordinate all laws on trafficking in persons and related offenses and the enforcement of those laws as well as adopting measures to increase the effectiveness of eradication of trafficking in persons.

According to NAPTIP News (2005/2006) Nigeria became the first African country to have a comprehensive anti human trafficking law and law enforcement Agency via NAPTIP. For her leading role in the war against trafficking in Africa, Nigeria's status of anti-trafficking was x-rayed at the 2004 international workshop on trafficking held in Accra, Ghana. As the only country in West Africa with a specific and uniform law on trafficking that is in consonance with the UN protocol and convention as well as the ECOWAS plan of action, Nigeria was recognized and asking to chair a session at that workshop (NAPTIP News 2005/2006).

In its bold steps towards actualizing the Agency's mandate which covers arresting, investigating and prosecuting traffickers, rescuing, rehabilitating and re-integrating victims of human trafficking, launching public enlightenment campaigns to sensitizing the people against the evil practices. The Agency (NAPTIP) with its pragmatic measures and approaches has recorded a good number of successes within a short time of operation which includes:

- Sensitization and awareness tours to trafficking endemic states and the establishment of advocacy groups in the affected states.
- Commissioning of national research projects on human trafficking.
- Mobilization of government bodies and stakeholders to join the efforts against Trafficking in persons.

- Establishment of National stakeholder consultative forum, made up of international organizations, government bodies and relevant non-governmental organization (NGOs), which meet quarterly to harness efforts in the fight against trafficking.
- Establishment of National investigation task force TIP.
- Establishment and management of rehabilitation shelters in Lagos and Benin in collaboration with international organization for migration (IOM).
- Production and airing of the agency's well packed jingle for awareness raising.
- Production and distribution of the trafficking in persons, prohibition Act and sensitization materials to the stakeholders and the public.
- Collaboration with foreign embassies and consulates in Nigeria and Nigeria foreign missions abroad.
- Implementing awareness campaigns and others and
- Rehabilitation of over 300 victims, most who have re-united with members of their families. Micro-credit facilities have been granted to various victims, and the agency monitors their progress. Some have also been re-integrated into schools (NAPTIP News Dec 2005-2006).

NAPTIP through collaborative efforts with other law enforcement agencies, international agencies, the Belgian and Italian governments has been able to reduce the incidences of the scourge. Hence, not less than 150 victims have been provided with receiving vocational training and scholarships (NAPTIP News 2005). However, through various international & local a shelter in Benin was established by international organizations in Nigeria (IOM) and supports from both the government of a United Stats of America and the federal government of Nigeria had also established another shelter in Lagos the shelters provide facilities for counseling, rehabilitation and re-integration of victims to the society.

With the efforts of NAPTIP, many countries such as the UK, Northern Ireland, Republic of Benin have all signed collaborative agreements with Nigeria. Also, there are some local Non-government organizations collaboration with NAPTIP in the light against the scourge of child abuse and human trafficking. They include WOTCLEF, IDIA, Renaissance, WOCON among others.

Due to the fact that there was no legal instrument for punishing offenders, NAPTIP took its notches higher by organizing a sensitization workshop for the Bar and the Bench, from 22 pilot project states, to educate and enlightened them on the new legal instrument, with the expectation that more offenders will soon find themselves in jail. All these laudable achievements are possible through the indefatigable efforts and leadership roles of Mrs. Carol Ndaguba the first Executive Secretary of NAPTIP.

From the foregoing the efforts of NAPTIP towards the fight, the crusade and eradication of the evils of man's inhumanity to man in the name of human trafficking and child labor are more recommendable. The Agency, no doubt, remains a role model in Africa. Though, the Agency has a lot of challenges to confront, yet they are equal to the task with the sincere assistance and cooperation of all citizens to finally put to an end this evil of modern day slavery: human trafficking and child labor.

In Nigeria, many organizations have taken it upon themselves to complement the efforts of the government of the day to total eradication of the cankerworm of child abuse and human Trafficking. To this effect, however, there have been massive crusades against these nefarious activities meted out to children by different Non- governmental Organizations (NGO'S) and International Organizations.

WOMEN TRAFFICKING AND CHILD LABOUR ERADICATION FOUNDATION (WOTCLEF)

In the Vanguard of the crusade against the devilish practice of child abuse and neglect, is the wife of the former Vice President of Federal Republic of Nigeria, Her Excellency, HAJIA TITILAYO AMINA ABUBAKAR, a woman of substance and a mother among mothers of our time. On her own, she has taken a grand step towards stalling the ugly trend by instituting a Non - governmental Organization a Women Trafficking And Child Labor Eradication Foundation' (WOTCLEF) which is now synonymous with the fight against women trafficking and child labor in Nigeria. It takes a great deal of time, resources and the rest to come up with the actualization of such an idea especially where the initiator is of great social, political, economic and religious relevance. It is praise - worthy that out of crowded schedule, Hajia Amina Abubarkar has been able to find time to come up with an idea that has benefited all and sundry.

The Women Trafficking and Child Labour Eradication Foundation (WOTCLEF) is an expression of Mrs. Abubarkar's unending feelings against man's inhumanity to man.

Formed in 1999, after the international workshop on National Centre for women trafficking and child labour migration which she organized in conjunction with the National centre for Women Development and Network for Poverty Alleviation and Sustainable Human Development, WOTCLEF has been able to champion the cause of humanity through the stallation of human trafficking either for prostitution, organ transplanting, child labour and other forms of economic exploitations within the shortest period . Her Excellency is a mother with the milk of human kindness flowing in her veins.

According to the Ibanga (2003), Mrs. Abubakar's aim was to ensure that the rights of trafficked persons are respected and protected by authorities and agencies.

OBJECTIVE OF WOTCLEF

- to place the Africa dimension of Trafficking and Child Labor on the global agenda for special attention and action
- To mobilize and motivate stakeholders atss all levels to respond to the challenge posed by trafficking, Child labour and violent abuses of the rights of women and children.
- To generate, organize and disseminate critical data and up to date information trafficking and child labour.
- To produce and public materials towards sensitization of the local, regional and global public about the problem.
- To rescue, rehabilitate and reintegrate victims into their communities in accordance with their best interests.
- To network and collaborate with concerned parties worldwide towards eradication of trafficking, Child labour and violent abuses of Women's Children's right
- To establish the WOTCLEF Rehabilitation and Special Purpose Centre in Abuja, Nigeria with Africa and worldwide affiliations.
- To establish special school programs for its catch them young' scheme.
- To work with relevant partners and concerned parities for the enactment and enforcement of appropriate legislation against trafficking, Child labor and violent abuses of the right of women and children.

Consequently, in her effort to promote child welfare, she painstakingly drafted and sponsored a bill on child trafficking to pursue adoption of laws and measures necessary to criminalize trafficking in human beings. According to Ibanga (2003) it is Mrs. Abubakar's conviction that there is a lacuna in the existing laws in the 1999 constitution. Although certain aspects of trafficking in human being are addressed, difficulties exist in their application, since it is not possible to prosecute the culprits on the corroborative testimony of one witness. This lacuna therefore was one of the factors that motivated her to sponsor a bill in 2001 known as 'National Agency for Trafficking in Persons' Law Enforcement and Administration Bill. To buttress her point, she said: if currency and drug trafficking could be tackled with specific legislation, why must similar laws not be enacted against the worst form of all trafficking - the human trafficking?

This bill, sponsored by Hajia Amina Abubakar will slam a jail term of ten (10) years of imprisonment and the forfeiture of property on offenders.

WOTCLEF as the foremost Non-governmental alternative to development has recorded a tremendous achievement in the areas of:

1. Creation of awareness about the evils of women trafficking and child labor.
2. Conducting massive campaigns in various part of the country through the distribution of printed materials, which speak against this social evil.

3. Education of youths on the dangers of child Trafficking, forced labor, and prostitution.

4. Sponsorship of radio - T V programs aimed at making the citizens to understand that woman Trafficking and child labor are never in the interest of the citizenry or the nation at large. Its social and economic implications are also made known to parents and the general public for them to be aware.

5. Cutting down the number of people who would have been infested with the dreaded HIV virus, which goes to explain her war against HIV/AIDS scourge. These achievements of Mrs Abubakar's pet project came on the heels of her determination to reform, and rehabilitate the victims.

6. Sponsorship of publications which wage war against sex export, child trafficking, child labor and other material which help in championing the interest of women and children.

7. Contribution of socio- economic growth of the polity through her effort at stopping shortage of Nigeria's future labour force children through her rehabilitation project.

8. WOTCLEF has succeeded in the restoration of societal values and has brought back the dignity of womanhood by laying more emphasis on the sanctity of women.

This pet -project of Hajia Abubakar, like a serious· mind. Really deserves every encouragement. However, this book is of the view that the grand actions and courage of Hajia Abubakar should be complemented.

All people of goodwill, governmental and non- governmental bodies and Agencies should wake up to the challenges thrown by WOTCLEF on this regard.

ROCHAS FOUNDATIONN COLLEGE

Owelle Anayo Rochas Okorocha is one of the most prominent, and inspiring personalities who buy out his time to champion the cause of the less privileged members of the society.

Yesterday, the was a monk with umbrella in the rain, but today, he is a high-heeled and well wired business mogul and colossus politician of our time inter alia the current. Special adviser to the president on inter-party Affairs. Owelle Anayo Rochas is a vibrant young man from a small town known as Ogboko in Ideato South Local Government Area of Imo State.

Born about 47 years ago, in Jos, Plateau State, the man, Owelle Anayo Rochas Okorocha has then the innate fire of patriotism and philanthropy burning in this heart at all times. He had thought of ways of touching the lives of the masses, especially the less privileged and vulnerable member of the society with a particular concentration on the development of children from indigent homes.

This wholesome wish of his, found expression in the establishment of the Rochas Foundation located along Okigwe Road, Owerri. It is on record that Owelle through this foundation has touched the lives of these vulnerable and handicapped groups by his aggressive and indiscriminate dishing out of both long term and short-term loans to members of the society; irrespective of socio-cultural and ethnic backgrounds.

Many a student has been able to complete their courses of study in different universities, polytechnics, colleges of Education and other tertiary institutions through this foundation.

People who had the intentions of going into one small scale business or the other but had no wherewithal to start off, finally found sponsorship in Rochas Foundation without being asked or requested to pay back. This in itself has contributed in no small measure to self-reliance and poverty reduction in Nigeria. Moreover, his desire to uplift the standard of living in the society has given birth to the establishment of a new household name, Rochas Foundation College, located along Onitsha Road, Owerri. This is a charitable institution committed to ensuring availability of education to the less privileged and orphans both single and double in the society. A man with much wisdom; he believes that education is the fundamental root and a sustainable economy as it is paramount in the growth and development of the nation at large.

The Rochas Foundation College is a qualitative and equipped secondary educational institute which offers free tuition, boarding, feeding, transportation, clothing and Medicare to the children of the poorest of the poor in Nigeria. The college has admitted a good number of students since its inception in the year 2001. Many children from less privileged homes and orphan have benefited immensely from this laudable project.

Owelle is a man whose veins flows with the "milk of human kindness" and believes in social justice; hence he often says:

"I see injustice and ask why not justice; I see poverty and why not affluence; I see the less privilege and I say why not Rochas Foundation; I see the children of the poorest of The poor unable to go to school and I say, why not Rochas Foundation college".

IDIA RENAISSANCE AND UNDERPRIVILEDGED TRUST FUND

Idia Renaissance and Underprivileged Trust Fund are two celebrated fontline Non-governmental organization in Edo State. These laudable ret project are the brainchild of a humble and diligent woman, and the wife of the former Edo State Governor, Mrs Ekinadosa Igbinedion. These projects were initiated and founded by Mrs Eginedion in 2000. It was her vision to restore and awaken the Edo women to the dignity of her past and upliftment of her cultural and moral value through Idia Renaissance. Also the underprivileged Child Trust fund was anchored on reclaiming the indigent children who are supposed to be in school acquiring education but rather hawking on the streets. It is (Mrs) Igbinedion's conviction that the talents that he latent within these bright but indigent children, their dreams and aspiration constitute an awesome pool of possibilities for the reconstruction of entire society when such sharp minds are not properly harnessed to contribute meaningfully to the growth and development of the nation.

In her observation, at the high rate at which Edo girls are being trafficked abroad for prostitution, (Mrs) Igninedion took it upon herself via Idia Renaissance to fight and eradicate the menace in Edo in her effort to emphasize the need to nip the menace in the bud, she asserted:

As a people we can no longer afford to turn a blind eye and watch our girls being sent to early graves through prostitution. Many of them return with deadly diseases that soon terminate their lives, leaving their wealth to others. It is the very reason why I have initiated the Idia Renaissance (Ibanga, 2001).

The organization has international mechanisms in its Networking activities fighting against human trafficking and prostitution.

Achievements Mrs Eki Igbinedion NGO's had an established model skills acquisition center that turns thousands of unskilled young girls into skilled and empowered citizens who can via industry, sustain and contribute meaningfully to alleviate the poverty of their homes. The NGO has been able to offer skill training in computer/Sec study fashion designing, home economies, costrietology as well as comprehensive counseling. On completion of the trainings and programs, the graduates give soft loans to set up their own small-scale business and thus become self-reliant.

Approximately, 5,000 young girls have benefited from this laudable project. In the area of the Underprivileged Children Trust Fund, the NGO had offered scholarship to a number of indigent children from the primary level of post primary level. Approximately 5,000 children have benefited from this project.

Eki is a mother of many virtues, humbly personified, kind and generous. A mother, who, despite her esteem, self, humbled herself to salvage the course of the underprivileged children and restore the dignity of womanhood in her state. Hence, she said.

I want to see a day when every underprivileged child gain education and the girl child in the state regain back the glories that projected Edo heroine like Emotan, Idia and the rest of them as women of dignity and pride.

THE ADOLESCENT PROJECT (TAP)

Justice (Mrs.) Mary Odili the amiable, a high court judge and the Wife of the former Executive Governor of Rivers State is one of the most prominent, active and inspiring personalities who champions the interest and welfare of the adolescents in our society. She is the initiator and founder of a non-government (NGO) known as the Adolescent project (TAP), a charitable organization aimed at empowering adolescents in Nigeria and Rivers State in particular.

TAP was founded in 1999. it is (Mrs.) Odili's vision to give back lost opportunity to the down-trodden and disadvantaged teenagers/adolescents in Rivers State.

She has the conviction that the adolescents potentiality and dynamism is high and, that they play significant role in all spheres of economic and social life, thus make vital contributions to the community's welfare assets adolescents suffer lack of access to productive assets and essential social services; and are often abused.

The objectives of TAP among others include:

(i) Making the highest possible individual development

(ii) To indicate leadership and responsive citizenship qualities in our adolescents while rescuing them from all pervading cankerworm of social malaise – child abuse, prostitution, human trafficking etc.

(iii) To improve the adolescents' access to education, skills acquisition credit and reproductive health services in order to enhance family well-being.

(iv) To reduce poverty, slow down population growth and ensure that natural resources are used prudently for sustainable national development.

ANCHORAGE OF TAP WITH GLOBAL VISION

TAP acts totally and thinks globally. The vision of TAP is in line with the UN millennium Development goals which include the:

1. Eradication of extreme poverty and hunger
2. Achievement of Universal Primary education.
3. Promotion of gender equality and empower women
4. Reduction of child mortality
5. Improvement of material wealth
6 Ensuring of environmental sustainability
7. Evolving a global partnership for development
8. Combat of HIV/Aids malaria and other diseases.

Tap has its activities gradually linked with other internal Non-governmental organizations via its networking mechanisms. One among others is the circle of hope sickle cell project London.

THE ACTIVITIES AND ACHIEVEMENTS OF TAP

Since its inception, TAP's foremost priority has reached out to teenage girls who are struggling with unplanned or unwanted pregnancy. Seen as a disgrace to their families once they get pregnant without being married, these teen ages are disowned and kicked out of their homes (Jama, 2003).

A trap has been providing succor to this dejected, rejected adolescent/teenagers. Through its adolescent center, it has provided skill acquisition, which had brought ethical rehabilitation of the underprivileged and abandoned adolescents. Thus, it provides both formal and informal education to enable young mothers and boys to help them who fall victims of abuse, become self sufficient and reliant. The boys who dropped out of school are habilitated and taught skills and courses in welding, auto repairs, carpentry, etc. On completion of their training, they are given the vocational tools to establish theirs.

Tap in its achievement has established approximately 7000 young people, mostly girls, have been helped through the program (Jama, 2003).

Furthermore, TAP via its awareness creation and outreach programs have representatives who move around the River from hamlets. They talk to traditional midwives in rural areas and teach them basic hygiene and primary health care practices to forestall both infant and material mortality rates and death resulting from birth complications.

Indeed, justice (Mrs) Odili is a rare gem among our political class using her intellectual and legal prowess borne out of her experience as a judge with moral lenses to reduce the number of potential nuisance among our youths, who may have ignorantly acquired such social status. Though a judge, she believes that all things are not to be viewed with legality alone, but that the plight of these vulnerable adolescence should also be examined with the moral conscience of mercy, compassion empathy and motherhood. She is really a woman of vision with a mission. A mother who shares the pains of the neglected, abandoned and the vulnerable group of adolescents in our society, always ready to descend the ladder of her exalted position to feel the pains of these young ones, to give them a sense of direction at a time it seems they apparently have none. TAP indeed deserves every support from all and sundry.

CHILD CARE TRUST (CCT)

The Child Care Trust (CCT) is not for profit non-organization. It is a private charitable foundation established. Her Excellency. Chief (Mrs.) Stella Obasanjo, former First Lady of the Federal Republic of Nigeria, to cater for the physically, socially and mentally challenged children in Nigeria. The Trust also runs a scholarship scheme for HIV/AIDS orphans, as well as rehabilitates abandoned babies in Nigeria.

The Child Care Trust is the result of a long-standing desire on the part of Chief (Mrs.) Stella Obasanjo to lighten the plight of persons with peculiar social, physical and mental challenges. This desire has been there, ever since she was old enough to realize that the disabled do not need our pity as much as they need our love and support.

The Trust is founded on the principle that when the necessary care and support are made available to a disabled child, he or she stands a reasonable chance of going on to lead a happier more fulfilling life as a worthy, productive and respected member of society.

Following the decision to establish the Child Care Trust, Chief (Mrs.) Stella Obasanjo visited several homes and hospitals in different parts of Nigeria, where disabled children are being rehabilitated. These visits revealed two facts. First, that challenged children can be as intelligent, talented and determined as other children. In other words, that, gives the required encouragement and assistance, the challenged child has just as much as potential for greatness as any other child. Secondary these visits exposed the deplorable state of many of the existing homes.

The Child Care Trust had designed its programs and projects to provide the needed educational and healthcare services for disabled children from birth to age 15. The Trust has built a center in Bwari, Abuja, Nigeria for children with special needs.

The Centre hosts a pre-primary and primary school, skills acquisition workshops, a fully equipped medical clinic and a computer/Internet center. Together, these facilities are designed to assist in providing specialized education and health care with the ultimate aim of equipping the children for life in the larger society. The Child Care Trust will, in its second phase development, establish similar homes in the six geopolitical zones of Nigeria to ensure that its programs reach more children in the rural areas of our country.

The goals of Child Care Trust include the following:

(a) The prevention of disability in children through immunization of children and women of childbearing age;

(b) The rehabilitation of children who have already suffered disability (including abandoned babies, who are said to be socially disabled) through the provision of special children model homes;

(c) Educating and training children, especially the disabled, in order to empower them to be self-reliant in the future;

(d) The provision of comprehensive medical services to children and the society at large;

(e) To train care providers from all over Nigeria to enable them cater better for the disabled;

(f) To maintain a databank on disability which will aid policy-making and planning for the disabled in Nigeria; and

(g) To enlighten the public to accept the disabled as human, and to end all forms of discrimination against them,

(h) To provide free education and other basic needs for socially challenged children, such as abandoned babies and HIV/AIDS orphans, we well as children infected by the HIV virus.

The above goals are achieved through three main programs, namely:

(a) Social Welfare Program;

(b) Medical Service Program; and

(c) Special Education Program; and

(d) The HIV/AIDS Orphans Scholarship Program

(a) The Social Welfare Program

Children who have already suffered disability need to be given hope and opportunity to be self-reliant in the future. This program aims at restoring hope and giving opportunity. Under this program, we maintain a rehabilitation home, called 'Special Children Model Home' for children.

Technical assistance in the form of food, drugs, consumables and money is also given to other rehabilitation homes and individuals in dire need in Nigeria, under this program. The special children model home is located at Child Care Trust Complex, Bwari, Abuja.

(b) The Medical Services Program

This program aims at providing comprehensive health care to children, especially the disabled. We have doctors, physiotherapists and nurses who handle the medical needs of children from within and outside the home. We have a fully equipped medical clinic at the CCT Complex, Bwari, Abuja.

Under the health program, immunization exercises against polio and other childhood killer diseases are carried out regularly in collaboration with the National Program on Immunization (NPI), as prevention is better than cure.

Drugs are also donated to public hospitals for the use of needy patients who cannot afford to pay for their drugs, under the technical assistance scheme.

We collaborate with National Hospital Abuja on referral and related matters.

(c) The Special Education Program

The Child Care Trust believes that quality education and skills acquisition are a prerequisite to the empowerment of children toward self-sustenance, aimed at poverty reduction. It also believes that educating the public will help in eliminating all forms of discrimination against the disabled. To this end, CCT runs the following under the Education Program:

(1) A nursery school for children ages 3-5 years;

(2) Primary school for children ages 6-11 years;

(3) Skills acquisition workshops for children ages 12 years and above;

(4) Care providers' Training for Nurses, Social Workers, Nannies, etc. Who cater for the challenged children.

(5) Public Enlightenment to educate the public on disability with a view to eliminating all forms of discrimination against the disabled; and

(6) Sponsorship for college and university, of disabled children who graduate from CCT schools for otherwise secure sponsorship under our scholarship scheme for orphans and vulnerable children.

The above facilities are open to children within and outside the CCT home for children with special needs.

Under the technical assistance scheme, books and other educational materials are also donated to special education centers, colleges, and universities to enrich their libraries.

The Nigerian government in the recent times through the joint task force of of the Nigerian military In June of 2013, the Borno state authorities set up a civilian militia, the Civilian Joint Task Force (CJTF). Their role is to assist the security forces in Borno state in order to identify and arrest Boko Haram members in the region.

According to the 2015 TIP Report the CJTF recruited and used child soldiers, sometimes by force. Although, the Government prohibited the recruitment and use of child soldiers and issued official statements condemning such use; the Borno state government continued to provide financial and in-kind resources to the CJTF

Other non-governmental Organization that has taken the matter of these unfortunate children under their care and has made much effort to give a worthwhile life includes, Child Labor Organization (CLO). African Network for the prevention and protection against Child Abuse and Neglect (ANPPCAN). International Society for the Prevention of Child Abuse and Neglect (ISPCAN), the child's lifeline CENTRE, the Bethesda child Agency, little saint orphanage, society against child abuse, society for prevention of cruelty to children etc.

RECOMMENDATION

Child abuse and Human Trafficking are serious offenses against humanity, hence the following recommendations are made:

I. The State Assemblies and the National Assembly should promulgate laws that would make child abuse a criminal offense A bill to guarantee the basic rights of children to good basic education, health care and freedom from all forms of abuse should be passed into law.

II. Government should beef up the poverty alleviation program is to create employment for the unemployed parents/guardians and give of free education to every Nigerian primary school.

III. There should be a legislation on the minimum age customary marriages and also proscribe some obnoxious cultural practices that are detrimental to the child welfare.

iv. The local councils should declare war against child abuse and Human Trafficking through an enlightenment campaign in their different locations. Social workers should be mobilized to monitor, care and report cases of child abuse and neglect.

v The law - makers should promulgate proper legislation that would circumscribe the activities of children street trading, hawking bus conductors etc.

VI The government should legislate on the number of children, hence family planning should be enforced.

vii The government should abolish all illegal motherless babies home, used as an outlet for the sale of babies and other forms of dehumanizing act.

viii The UNITED NATIONS should proscribe the adoption of children in the army or guerilla during the war in any African country.

ix. The government should provide rehabilitation centers and homes of victims of violence.

CONCLUSION

Child abuse and human trafficking are problems that need urgent attention. In Nigeria society, the problem of Child Abuse and Human Trafficking has not been given adequate attention, there is an absolute disregard for the welfare of children in spite of the fanfare that attends the birth of a new child.

Though some special days have been observed for children recognition such as May 27 (Children's day), October 1st Universal Children's day, June 4 International day for Innocent Children Victims of aggression, June 16 African Children's Day. The society no doubt lends weight behind the observation of these important days in the life of every Nigerian child. Yet the African child, and indeed Nigerian Child, suffers in the midst of plenty (Ahiante, 2000).

The society should shun violence against children and work towards their upliftment. The future of this country, Nigeria, lies in these children. The society should be a watchdog and report every crime against children no matter whose ox is gored. Martin Luther King Once remarked, "The World is full of evil today not because of men who do evil; but because of men who keep silence and watch evil being done".

The recommendation given in this text, if properly implemented, would definitely promote a child's welfare in the society. The parents Guardian, society and government at all levels should reassess their views on children and the status they are being given in order to work for their betterment.

Finally, every member of the society is enjoined to fight child abuse and human trafficking in our children and make the welfare of these children their business. These should be done to forestall the ever-increasing rate of maladjustive behavior and violence, which characterized many youths today, thus ensuring global peace. All hands must be on deck to combat these cankerworms in our society.

REFERENCE

Ayo Ouajobe Better Protection for Women And Children Under The Law In Bola Ajibola (1989) Women and Children Under Nigeria Law, Lagos: The Federal Ministry of Justice.

Achebe, C. (1958) Things Fall Apart, Ibadan Heinemann Educational Books.

Adenuga R.A. (2000) panacea to Child Labor and Abuse Journal of Education Focus: Institute of Education Ogun State Nigeria Vol. 2 No 2 June.

Ajomuo M.A. (1993) Individual Rights Under The 1989 Constitution. NIAL Lagos.

Ahiante A. (2000 June 16) "weep not, African Child" This day.

Ahiante A. (2000 June is improving the right of the Africa Child Thisday

Akarue, J. (2004:June) "Ghana Castle of no return" New Africa Magazine.

Berger Report "Report of The Royal Commission on Family and Children Law at Eekalaar J. (1978) Family Law and Social Policy London Wadein Fall and Nicolsons.

Callaway A.C. (1981) Drop Out From Nigeria School 1961-1971 Ibadan: Niser.

Chase N.F :A Child Being Beaten" In Shepard J.M. (1978) Sociology, California.

Constitutional Right Project (1999) Lagos.

Donli H.N. "Socio-Legal Consequences of Child Abuse" In Bola Ajibola (Ed 1989) Women and Children Under Nigerian Law Lagos: Federal Ministry of Justice

Dennis, O. O. [2004] 'Human Trafficking, Bane of societal development' Dialogue, April 2004.

Eekalaar J. (1978) Family Law and Social Policy London; Weiden field and Nicolson.

Encyclopedia Britannica (1974) Vol.16 Helen Hemington Chicago: Benton publisher.

Evelyn Sharp (1920) The African Child an Account of the International Conference of African Children Geneva: Connection Negro University Press.

Fayoyin A (1993) the Menace of VVF in VVF in Nigeria Population quarterly Journal of Population activities in Nigeria Oct-Dec. 1993 Ahiante A (2000, June 16) This Day.

Funke Egbemode (2000: July 30) Punch (Nig) Ltd. Lagos

Hall E. (1982) Child Psychology today. New York: London House.

Gray D. Turning out: A Study of Teenage Prostitution" in Stark, R (1987) Sociology, 2nd edition California Wadsworth Publishing Co.

Harry G. (1979) Abnormal Psychology: A Community Mental Health perspective. Chicago: Science research associates, Inc.

Ibanga; V. (2002 April 21) Fight against human trafficking Daily champion.

Kaita H.I. "Women's Education in Nigeria" in Adaralegbe A (1969) A Philosophy for Nigeria Education Ibadan. Heinemann Education Books (Nig) Ltd.

Lass Well M. and T. Lass well (1987) Marriage and the family to the competence in children in Laswell M & Lasswel T. (1987) Marriage and the family California Wadsworth Inc.

NPC/UNICEF (2001) Children and Women's Right in Nigeria. A wake-up call situation assessment and analysis NPC/UNICEF Abuja.

Nigel Parton (1985) The Politics of Child Abuse: London Macmillan Education Limited.

Njoku, N.L. (1998) studies in Western imperialism and African Development, Owerri. Tony Ben publishers.

Okeke C. (2003) philosophy of education, concepts Analysis and application Owerri Design publishers.

Oketunbi J. (2000. June 21) The guardian

Osauzo T (2003: Sept 25) Rejected Old man Bathes teenage girl with acid Daily Sun.

Olaoye (2000: April 26) How Aids Destroys Children. National Post

Ogbeh. (2001: February, 7) Children's Special Session on rights of the Child Vanguard.

Ogundipe, A, (2004: April) "Good moral values and Reorientation will check women trafficking in Dialogue.

Oriakhi, F. (2004, April 19) "Of the children and women trafficking Guardian.

Obadina, T. (2001, Dec.) "Modern slavery and Economic Development in Africa today magazine.

Osuafor, C. and Njoku, N.L. (1995) Africa: Making whole again. Owerri, Name Ventures Nig Ltd.

Rodney Stark (1987) Sociology) 2nd Ed) California Wadsworth Publishing Co.

Reece Megee J. (1980) Sociology: An Introduction New York; Holt Rimehart and Winston.

Ray. C. (2005, Jan) "The origins of mixed Race Populations" New African magazine.

Salami S.O. "Etiology, treated and prevention of Juvenile delinquent among Nigeria School going Adolescent in Ogunlade E.O. Et al (1977) Kontagora Journal of Education.

The Punch (1999: June 14) |Children Under Arms" Punch (NIG) LTD Lagos.

Uzoigwe, G.N. (1973) the Slave Trade and Africans Societies in Transactions of the History Society of Ghana. Vol x iv, No 12 pp 187, 212

United Nations Cited in Dialogue April 2004 Ehigiamusoe, G. (2004, April) Trackling Female traffics an unpopular Approach in Dialogue April 2004.

Women's Centre for Peace and Development (Woped) (2000) The bane of our times; A fact file on cases of violence against Women and Girls in Nigeria WOPED publication: Lagos.

Webster's New Encyclopedic Dictionary (1995) New York: Black Dog and Leventhal publishers Inc.

World Book (2001) World Book, Inc Chicago

Okafor f.c Philosophy of education, cold third world Perspective in Okeke C (2003) philosophy of Education concepts Analysis and application Owerri. Design publisher.

Olawale R. (2000 Sept 11) "Child Labor: Enterprise that demeans the nation" The Guardian.

Aina Y. (2000 July 21) saving the African Child from traffickers" Punch.

Olusola A. 2000 May 25, the African Child and invisible slavery, Vanguard.

Mudiaga Ofuoku (1999-July 26) sex Export" in Newswatch Ikeja News Watch Communication Ltd.

Odudu Okponegete (1999, Feb 9) Dangers of poor childhood education. National post.

Odoemenan, S. (1994 July 3-6) The need to evolve services for crime victims. National Ambassador.

Jama T. A. (2003) "Rape of innocence" in News Africa November 30

Ebhodaghe.S. (2000, Feb. 18) "A Man's Inhumanity to a girl" The Guardian.

Nigeria". *Trafficking in Persons Report 2010*. U.S. Department of State (June 14, 2010)

Human Rights Watch. World Report2015:Nigeriahttps://www.hrw.org/world-Report/2015/country-chapters/Nigeria

Assume oh & Enabunene Sylvester, "Women Trafficking and Violations of Right to Life in Nigeria", Online Journal of Social Sciences Research, 2012, Volume 1, Issue 2, pp. 62-68

United States Department of State, Office To Monitor and Combat Trafficking in Persons, 2015 Trafficking in Persons Report –Nigeria.

Monica Imam, "Human trafficking and HIV/AIDS" paper presented at a two day workshop organized by NAPTIP/UNDP (2010) on the danger of child trafficking in Nigeria at Zaranda hotel Bauchi, Bauchi State.

Ejike Leadership Newspaper of 4thDecember, 2014.

Printed by Books on Demand GmbH, Norderstedt / Germany